Nasturtiums for Grandma Minnie

By Kathy Harding

Nasturtiums for Grandma Minnie

By Kathy Harding

ISBN-13: 978-1466334649
ISBN-10: 1466334649

Dedication

I dedicate this labor of love to my mom. I could not have written it without her knowledge and help. Thank you, mom for your unconditional love, support and guidance through the years. Thank you for always believing in me and never doubting my dreams. Thank you for sharing your love and appreciation for family, God and life itself. You sacrificed so much for us and it's impossible to thank you adequately for everything you've done. I could not ask for a better parent or role model. I love you.

And to Grandma Leda, I know you're in a better place now, but I love and miss you dearly. Thank you to my husband, Mike for your love and encouragement while I was working on this project and neglecting the dirty dishes! I love you for your support. Thank you to Sam and Tim. You guys are the greatest kids and I write this book for you and the kids you'll have one day. Be proud of who you are. I love you both more than words can say.

"Mothers hold their children's hands for just a little while, and their hearts forever." Old Irish proverb.

ACKNOWLEDGMENTS

Thank you Edna Nickell, Grace Nordang, Hazel Newman, Gayle Thrapp, Bill Brownlee and Margaret Farley for providing me with help and information needed to complete this book. Thank you also, Betty McKee, Sandy Hill and my brother, Kevin Hixon for your help and support.

CONTENTS

1 The Manor

It was the spring of 1908. The stately Victorian twenty-three room, 13,000 square foot mansion, known as Flat Top Manor, stood high on the side of the mountain surrounded by 3,600 acres of forest. The mighty white dwelling, belonging to the Moses Cone family, required various servants to cook, clean and maintain the spacious home. The beautiful gardens, apple orchards and well manicured grounds surrounding the mansion also required gardeners and other such laborers to maintain its pristine and beautiful appearance. The mansion was named Flat Top Manor because of its nearness to Flat Top Mountain, which the Cone family also purchased in 1899. Both Grandfather Mountain, located a few miles south, and Flat Top Mountain are all part of the Blue Ridge Mountains range.

Built by the Cone family, the mansion was a sense of pride in the community, although most in the small town of Blowing Rock, North Carolina were poor and lived very simple and humble lives in their modest homes. Jobs were scarce, so the mansion provided much needed employment for the fortunate few lucky enough to be hired by the Cone family to tend to the sprawling estate. The Cones added three lakes and stocked them with trout and bass. The local farmers whose farms were now a part of the Cone estate were allowed to stay and many were hired as tenants of the estate. The estate had many apple orchards, and there were many barns on the property to sort and process the apples, which also provided jobs to the community. The Cones also raised sheep, making it not just a summer retreat but a year round working business.

Moses Cone, son of Jewish-German immigrants, was a man in his fifties. He wore his dark hair parted down the middle and sported a handle bar mustache. He was quiet, kind, small in stature and had a soft pleasant voice. Cone made his fortune in the textile industry making denim material for manufacturers, including Levi Strauss and then settled in the Blue Ridge Mountains near Blowing Rock with his wife, Bertha. With so much to offer, many who knew them thought it tragic they never had children to share in their great fortune.

The Cones had many visitors to the estate during the summer months. Family and friends from Baltimore often escaped the heat of the city and retreated to Flat Top Manor. Bertha Cone's unmarried sisters, Sophie and Clementine Lindau visited the mansion often. Moses Cone's brother, Ceasar and his family also visited, as did his art collector sisters, Claribel and Etta. It would seem the manor was full most of the summer months. The third floor attic housed a kitchen and living quarters for nannies and servants who looked after the children of their guests.

Minnie Lee Coffey was one of the fortunate few who worked for the Cones. She was a fine cook and the Cones considered her a great asset and a reliable employee. Minnie was a soft spoken eloquent young lady of seventeen years old. She was tall for a woman of her day, and had a slim build, a quick smile and keen sense of humor. Like her sisters, and most of the women of her day, her long brown hair was always worn up in a bun and off her shoulders. Minnie loved to laugh, she loved life, and everyone who knew her appreciated her kindness, fondness for living and her love for people. She was the youngest living child of eight children, born to Gilliam and Sarah Jane Coffey on July 31, 1890 in Blowing Rock, Watauga Township, North

Carolina. Gilliam and Sarah Jane also had a daughter named Ethel, but she died as an infant. Minnie had four surviving sisters and two brothers. They were a hard working family, but not dirt poor like so many were in those days. Still, they appreciated the value of a dollar and were no stranger to an honest day's work. Minnie's father, Gilliam owned more than fifty acres of farm land in the mountains near the community of Blowing Rock, North Carolina. In that respect, they were far from poor in a time where many of their neighbors had very little.

Both of Minnie's grandfathers fought in the civil war, wearing the gray uniform of the Confederate army. Her father's father, Larkin Coffey died of typhoid fever during an outbreak while stationed with his unit in the Cumberland Gap. He was buried in Lafollette, Tennessee. Her mother's father, Joseph Isenhour, survived the Civil War. Times were hard, and the Confederate dollar was worthless. He sold his holdings in the flat land and moved to the mountains to live near his daughter, Sarah Jane and her family. Before he moved, however, he gave a plot of ground to the negro couple who had been with his family for many years. The negro slave known as Aunt Rose, and her husband had been given to Joseph's wife, Letitia by her parents as a wedding gift. After the war, they had stayed on the farm and worked for wages.

Gilliam Coffey's ancestors arrived in America in about 1772. They were farmers who hailed from Killucan, Westmeath County, Ireland. North Carolina seemed to be the popular destination for Coffeys leaving Ireland, as so many of them immigrated to the state. Gilliam had deep roots in North Carolina, so the family never considered living anywhere else. That is, not until the spring of 1908.

Blowing Rock was chartered and incorporated on March 11, 1889. Prior to incorporation, Fort Rollins, a Civil War post was located there. The Greene, Coffey, Bolick, Estes, Hayes and Storie families were the first to settle in Blowing Rock in the mid 1860's.

There was talk in the family of moving west. Minnie's sister, Candus and her husband, Lee Cook had ventured out to the Pacific Northwest state of Washington in 1901 to farm. Eventually they had their own farm and apple orchard establishing themselves in a community known as Spring Coulee near the small town of Okanogan, Washington. In 1906, her sisters Julia and Cordie moved to the same area with their husbands. Minnie knew they would probably never return to Blowing Rock, not to live anyway.

Moving away from the only home she ever knew was a bit daunting to Minnie, yet since she had never traveled far from Blowing Rock, she was also curious about seeing new places and experiencing different cultures. Whether to move, or not, would be a difficult decision to make once the time came. Candus had sent her a post card of three Indian women that fascinated Minnie. She was curious about the west, just not so sure she wanted to live there. After all, she still had a fondness for North Carolina and did not see a reason to leave it behind for good.

The late spring mornings were still cool as Minnie took her daily stroll on the grounds surrounding the mansion. She lived in one of the larger out buildings located on the estate. Her quarters were plain but clean and new. A few of the other female servants also lived in this building which housed the laundry facilities. Washing clothes, however, was not Minnie's responsibility. She was the Cone's private cook, and she was available to prepare three meals a day for Moses and Bertha Cone.

Minnie enjoyed seeing her uncle Tilden who made a daily ritual of meeting her in front of the mansion to start her morning. Solomon Tilden Isenhower was her mother's half brother. He had worked as a gardener at the mansion since it was built and helped Minnie acquire her cooking job there. Tilden's wife, Callie had a family connection to the manor too. Her brother, Arthur C. Moody was in charge of the manor as the general manager and head caretaker of the grounds. John Nelson Coffey, Minnie's father's brother also worked at the manor. John was a farmer and a shoe maker but worked on the estate part time. He had various jobs from planting apple trees to keeping poachers out of Moses Cone's trout and bass lakes. Yet another Coffey worked at the manor as well, his name was Austin Blaine Coffey. His grandfather and Minnie's grandfather were brothers.

"Good morning, Minnie," Tilden said with a smile as he approached her.

"Ah, Uncle Tilden, what a beautiful crisp morning it is," she replied as she secured the shawl around her shoulders. "I'm so glad to be back to work and staying at the manor again. I certainly miss this place during the winter months."

Tilden smiled. "It's good to have the summer crew back. I've missed everyone. It's still cool, alright, but it won't be long until we'll be griping about the heat."

"How are you today, Uncle Tilden? And how is Aunt Callie?" she asked.

"I'm upright and ready to work. God has blessed me today. Callie says she misses you. You should stop and see her soon."

"I believe I will. Seems lately I've been so busy, but I must make a point to go see her. You best get to those roses, they are starting to grow already and your brother in law might have to get after you!" Minnie teased as she climbed the many stairs to the mansion's front porch.

"Yeah, that Arthur is a scary fellow!" Tilden teased. "See you later today, Minnie. Take care now."

Minnie waved to Tilden, and then made her way into the manor, greeting the hired help along the way to the large dining area located at the front of the home. She exchanged her shawl on the coat rack for her apron and tied it behind her as she approached the kitchen.

The aroma of frying bacon and coffee brewing soon filled the house as it did every morning. Moses and Bertha Cone would soon be down from their huge bedroom suite dressed and ready to start their day with a hearty hot breakfast. Minnie's day was very regimented, breakfast at seven o'clock, lunch at noon and dinner at six o'clock.

Minnie served the Cones as soon as they took their seats at the table. She would first serve coffee, and then their meal.

Moses sipped from the cup. "Good morning, Minnie, how are you today?" he asked with his usual friendly smile.

"I'm fine, sir. It's a beautiful spring morning, isn't it?"

The Cones were always pleasant enough to all of the staff, but they had a special fondness for Minnie. Bertha Cone would often visit with her on her work breaks and they would have coffee together.

After breakfast, it was Moses Cone that found Minnie sitting at the table in the large dining room. The room was spacious and adequate enough to comfortably host several people when the Cones chose to have guests for dinner parties. The front wall of the dining area was covered with windows that over looked the grounds. Minnie was sitting in the sunlight, intently reading a letter when he quietly approached her.

"Excuse me, Minnie. Do you have time to talk awhile? I don't want to intrude upon your break," he said.

Minnie gently folded the letter and put it back inside the envelope.

"Please, sit down. You're not intruding at all. I was reading a letter from my sister, Candus. She and her husband, Lee have a farm and apple orchard in Washington State. My sisters Cordie and Julia live there too."

"Yes, your uncle Tilden told me about your sisters living in the northwest. Actually, that's one thing I wanted to talk to you about."

"Is something wrong?" Minnie asked as Moses sat down on the chair across the table from her.

"Oh no, nothing is wrong exactly. Tilden is a good man, and he's been with me for a while now. Likewise, you are very valuable to us in so many ways. Tilden tells me your family is considering joining your sisters in Washington. Is this true?"

"Well, I don't know. It's something we've been asked to consider," she paused. "I am not sure if all of us are ready to sell our homes and move clear across the United States. What if we get out there and don't like it? It would be hard to just come back home. That's a far piece to travel and expensive too, just to pack up and move like that."

"Yes, yes it is. I hope you don't leave us, Minnie. But if you do, I wish you well. You're a fine person and you are an asset to Bertha and me. We would hate to see you go but if you ever need references, I'd be glad to help. Naturally I was curious if you were truly planning on leaving us."

"Mr. Cone, I don't see us moving anytime soon. So don't you worry. I'll be here for a while yet, I promise," Minnie replied with a reassuring smile.

Moses stood up, pushed his chair under the table and smiled. "It's so good to see you again, Minnie. I trust you and your family made it through the winter alright?"

"Yes, we had a very nice Christmas and winter went well. It's good to see you and Mrs. Cone again too. It's good to be back to work again."

"It's good to be home again," Moses chuckled. "I love Baltimore, but I truly miss this place when we are gone. See you at lunch time, Minnie. Well, I'm headed to China this morning."

"China?" Minnie asked.

"Oh yes, that's the apple orchard farthest from the house. It's so far away, it's as though it's on the other side of the world when you go to walk out there, so we refer to it as China," he joked.

"Very clever," Minnie replied.

Minnie smiled as Moses turned to walk away. She pulled the letter from the envelope and soon was lost again in the words she read. Candus had a way with words and Minnie was always entertained by her letters. As much as she loved Blowing Rock, the thought of a new place and a new beginning intrigued Minnie. If nothing else, she certainly enjoyed reading about it.

2 Sunday Dinner With Jake

On Saturdays, Minnie prepared the Cone's breakfast and lunch and then had much of the weekend off, unless of course, they happened to be entertaining guests for a meal. She often spent her free time with her folks surrounded by brothers and a sister who also took advantage of their time away from work to visit the family. Her Uncle Tilden, Aunt Callie and their children Frank, Charlie, Texie, Geneva and Louise would often visit them as well. Callie was her aunt, but they were close like sisters, despite their eleven year age difference.

Minnie loved the special time with her large family and often wondered what she would do if they all were to move far away from the only place she had ever called home. She could not allow them to move without her. She could not bear being without Mama and Papa, for sure. But how could she move so far away from Callie? It was not easy adjusting to life without her sisters, but it was interesting to hear of their adventures in a place so unlike her home in Blowing Rock.

And then there was the subject of Jake. Although Jake and Minnie were considered courting, Minnie did not consider Jake a serious beau. She did consider him a good friend, however, and would miss Jake if she left Blowing Rock. Minnie was a popular and pretty young lady with several suitors, but Jake was special. She always figured once she was ready to marry, Jake might be the one.

Minnie was a lady of many talents and she loved to sing with her church choir. She was self taught on guitar and enjoyed playing when time permitted. She also had a reputation for her pleasant singing voice. Jake was proud of her talents and bragged about her to everyone who would listen. He was very attentive and often doted on Minnie. He would tell his friends that Minnie sang like an angel.

Minnie and her family were members of the local Southern Baptist church. Minnie's faith was very important to her, so she rarely missed a Sunday church service. Jake would always meet up with her and sit with the family.

Minnie and a small group of friends performed for their church family nearly every Sunday. Her alto voice carried the small choir as she sang for the Lord. Their angelic voices filled the high ceiling of the church building with praise and admiration. Everyone looked forward to their weekly performance. Jake was proud and sat tall with a smile on his face as he watched and listened to Minnie sing. He did not see the other young ladies, he only had eyes for Minnie.

On Sunday after church, the family usually gathered at Gilliam and Sarah Jane's home on Shulls Mills Road for a meal. Larkin and Emma lived thirty miles away, so it was not always feasible for them to travel the far distance by horse and wagon with their baby, Ethel. Minnie loved having the entire family together when possible. Since Jake was considered family, he enjoyed escorting her home from church and would stay for the meal.

Today the family was gathered for the Sunday meal and this made Sarah Jane very happy and content. She set enough dishes on the long table to accommodate everyone, adult children, their spouses, grandchildren and Jake. Minnie always sat with Jake to her right, and Papa on her left. Everyone quickly scurried to sit at the table, and as always, it was a tight squeeze, elbow to elbow but no one seemed to mind. The important thing was, they were together as they prayed over their meal. The only thing missing from the table that day were their three daughters, Candus, Cordie, Julia and their families.

Coincidentally, three of the sisters had husbands with the surname Cook. Cordie's husband, Walter Cook and Candus's husband, Lee Cook were cousins but Martha's husband, Hoyt Cook was not related to the other two men.

Gilliam picked up the platter of chicken, forked a piece and dropped it to his plate then passed it on to Sarah Jane.

"Ya did good, ma." He proclaimed. "I'm starving."

Sarah Jane smiled and took a piece of chicken from the plate.

"Nothing like a beautiful sunny Sunday to get the appetite going," she said as she passed the chicken on to her son, Larkin. "I'm glad you all are here today."

She paused and looked around the table at everyone like she had something to say.

"We're happy to be here, Mama," Larkin replied.

"Is there something wrong, Mama?" Martha asked.

Sarah Jane smiled and shook her head no.

"No, nothing is wrong, daughter. But I feel we do need to talk about our future here in Blowing Rock."

The brothers and sisters glanced at one another as the food continued being passed around the table. They knew this conversation was inevitable.

Larkin looked over at Minnie and then Martha. He glanced over at his brother, Joe, looking for any kind of reaction from anyone. Larkin's wife, Emma squeezed his hand as it lay on her lap.

"So, is this going to be the conversation at the supper table today?" Joe asked.

Gilliam cleared his throat and surveyed the faces before him at the table. Everyone was still and stared back at him, waiting for an answer.

"I won't consider such a move if the rest of you aren't up to it," Gilliam said. "But if ya'll are thinking it might be a good thing, we need to have a plan. I know there's a lot to consider because of them we might leave behind. I have my family here too and it won't be easy leaving them, but if that's what we decide is best for this family, I will consider it."

"It will take time, there's no way ya'll could sell your places and move inside a year's time," Joe replied. "That is, if you even want to sell. Maybe not all of us want to leave. What makes living out there any better than what we have right here?"

Martha, known affectionately by the family as Matt, quickly reached for her glass of water and took a sip. "I agree. Are we so sure we really want to move?" she asked. "Hoyt and me aren't so convinced it would be a good thing to do. Well, I'm not so sure but Hoyt seems to think we should stay."

Not wanting to get in a clash with the family, Hoyt shook his head in support of his wife, but continued eating his chicken without saying a word.

Larkin scooped up a spoonful of mash potatoes, slapped it on his plate and passed the bowl to Jake. "Emma and I are ready for a change," he said. "I say we should go. Besides, I miss my sisters."

"I miss them too, and I think I'd like to go," Minnie agreed. "But what happens if we get all the way out there and hate it, then what?"

Gilliam sucked a piece of chicken from his teeth and slowly wiped his lips with his napkin.

"Alright then," he paused. "I see we aren't all on board with this move and have some apprehensions. I reckon we shouldn't try to be in a hurry about this decision. It's a two year plan at best. But, I'd like us to consider going as a family."

In disbelief, Jake glanced over at Minnie. She never discussed a possible move with him. She did not want him to fret over something that might not ever happen. Now it was out there for him to digest. Needless to say, he was shocked to hear such news. Minnie had always wanted to tell him in her own way, but there never seemed to be the right moment to break the news.

Minnie dropped her head, avoiding eye contact with Jake. She did not know what to say to him. He obviously did not know what to say to her either, as he remained speechless. Hurting Jake was the last thing she wanted to do.

Gilliam noticed Jake's reaction and smiled. "Jake, my boy, don't look so forlorn. At this rate, it may never happen, and it certainly won't happen tomorrow." he reassured. "Now eat your chicken and don't fret none."

The family finished their meal without another word about moving west. Jake was very quiet, which was out of character for him. He enjoyed interacting with the family very much and they always made him feel as if he was already a part of the family. He always looked forward to the Sunday meal and time spent visiting with Minnie and her family.

After the meal, the men folk would gather on the front porch as the women cleared the table and washed up the dishes. Minnie would always hurry to do her part so she could spend time with Jake. Today, however, was different. She dreaded the confrontation with Jake regarding all the big plans he was privy to at the supper table.

Once her kitchen chores were complete, Minnie found Jake standing near the barn visiting with Larkin. She slowly walked up to them while rehearsing what she wanted to say to Jake playing over in her head.

"Lark, can I speak to Jake alone?" she asked.

"Why don't you just marry the guy, Minnie, and we'll take him with us!" Larkin said with a snort to his laugh.

"William Larkin Coffey, you mind your manners," Minnie responded. "Now get on out of here so I can have a word with Jake."

Larkin smiled, slapped Jake on the shoulder to show his support and left them alone to talk.

Jake stared at the ground, waiting for Minnie to speak first. Minnie stared at the top of his head, waiting for the right words to come to mind.

"Jake, this isn't a done deal you know. It's just a lot of talk," she finally said.

"I think if it's something your mama wants, it's going to happen sooner or later," he replied still looking at the ground.

"Jake, look at me." Minnie touched the bottom of his chin and gently pulled his face up so she could look into his eyes. "I can't promise you it won't happen, but what if it doesn't? All that worry will be for nothing."

"If we got married, Minnie, would you stay in Blowing Rock then?" Jake asked with some frustration to his voice.

Minnie was taken aback by such a bold question! Jake had never mentioned marriage before. It was obvious to her, however, this option was offered to her out of sheer desperation. She paused to regain her thoughts and composure.

"Jake, I do think you care for me. And I care for you too, but perhaps not in that way. I don't think you're truly ready to marry me or you'd have asked already. Don't ask me to marry you until you ask me for the right reasons and it comes from your heart."

"You know we'll be married one day, Minnie. I'd marry you now to keep you from moving," he replied.

"No, Jake. There's no hurry. Let's just see what God has in store for us. Don't you fret now, if we're meant to be together, that's what will happen."

Jake hugged Minnie and kissed her cheek. At that moment, Minnie felt she was losing a good friend and was a little sad. She knew deep down in her soul that she could very well move away from Blowing Rock one day. For now, it was all in God's hands.

Life in the Blue Ridge Mountains went on as usual. Jake saw Minnie when time permitted, but Minnie felt their relationship was never quite the same after that Sunday when Papa spilled the beans about the potential big move to the west.

3 Sad News At The Manor

Soon the cool spring turned into an unusually warm and humid summer. The mountains were known for their mild temperatures, so this weather took some getting use to. A part of Minnie hoped moving was a fading notion for her folks. However, the adventurous part of her personality was still open to the idea of such a move, despite how disappointed Jake would be if it happened.

Candus and Lee seemed to be doing well in Washington State. Minnie looked forward to every letter her sister wrote. Candus was very reliable about writing to the family and keeping them informed of their lives in the Northwest, but in recent months it was evident she was more desperate for the family to consider a move to join them in the west.

Unfortunately, Candus and Lee were unable to have children of their own. In 1901 they took in a foster child named Ruie Hollis Cook and took her west to Washington with them. Having no children of their own was a large void in their lives, but caring for seven year old Ruie helped to make up for the need of raising a child of their own. Ruie's father was Leland Cook, but it was never clear why he was unable to raise his daughter on his own. Never the less, she needed a home and Candus and Lee needed a child. Coming from a large family herself, Candus felt the need for children and this was an opportunity to give this little girl a proper home. Candus never regretted the move west, but underestimated just how much she would miss her family. She was determined to convince them all to make the move west as well.

Sarah Jane was already convinced, and she was ready for the move. She missed her daughters very much, but was not keen on leaving the rest of her children behind. Soon, there would be more grandchildren to consider. Cordie and Julia had eight kids between them already and Sarah Jane desperately wanted to know them. Julie's children were Charles, Cecil, Velma, Rufus and Tessie. Cordie had Grady, Oscar, and Hazel. The only grandchildren she really knew were Larkin and Emma's little Ethel, and Martha's girls, Velma and Grace. Knowing there would be more grandchildren, Sarah Jane could not accept the idea of never knowing them all. She lived for the day her home was full of grandbabies to spoil and love. She wanted them to be a big part of her life.

Minnie began taking her breaks on the mansion's front steps. Being outside in the fresh air was a welcome relief from the hot stove in the kitchen. She appreciated the cool mountain breezes that blew through. At times Tilden would join Minnie on the steps and commiserate on how warm the day was, when in fact, Blowing Rock had some of the most mild summer temperatures in all of the south. Callie and her children would sometimes ride out to the mansion to visit with them both. She would bring sandwiches and drinks and they would sit in the shade of the oak tree to visit and have lunch together before going back to work. Sometimes they would even ask Callie's brother, Arthur Moody to join them on their picnics.

Callie and Minnie could visit and laugh for hours. Callie's given name was Caledonia Ruth Moody born September 9, 1879. They were kindred spirits, and Minnie knew it would be very difficult to leave her behind. She would miss her and Tilden very much if the family moved away. Minnie's friends Laura and John Moody were also very special to her. They were a married couple and the same age as Minnie. John was a cousin to Callie. How difficult it would be to up and leave all her friends and family, maybe never to see them again.

When time permitted, Minnie grabbed her large sun bonnet and ventured outdoors to the garden area. She enjoyed helping in the Cone's vegetable garden. She picked the vegetables she would later prepare for their meals, but she also enjoyed working the soil and pulling the pesky weeds that insisted on taking over the large well manicured garden. Occasionally, Bertha Cone would help her in the garden. She too had a passion for gardening and Minnie enjoyed her company.

Minnie also had a love for flowers, she enjoyed helping care for the vast varieties of flowers the Cones had growing on their estate. Tilden welcomed her help, and Minnie learned a lot about the knack of growing roses from him. He was pleased she took such an interest in the vegetable and flower gardens, as it gave him more time for chores he was more suited for, the larger bushes, shrubs and trees on the estate. Tilden was well known for his talents with landscapes and grooming. He took pride in his work as he looked at it all through the eyes of a perfectionist.

Jake still made an occasional appearance at the mansion to visit, but not as frequently as he had in the past. He never missed a church service, however, he stopped having Sunday meals with the Coffeys. Minnie did not mind that she saw less of Jake, although she was still very fond of him. Weaning himself away from her and the family now might be a good thing, as one day he might have to say goodbye to her for good.

The warmer month of August soon turned into a much more reasonable month of September. For the months that followed, Minnie's life was busy with family and social activities. In October, the trees in the valley below the mansion turned brilliant orange, maroon and yellow. Minnie often stood at the edge of the estate's lawn, high atop the mountain, and looked down at the fish stocked lake below surrounded by all the magnificent autumn colors. The spectacular view was breathtaking. Minnie felt fortunate to witness such a beautiful transformation of nature. How could any place on earth be better than this? She wondered how she could even consider leaving this place.

Soon the Cones would be leaving the mansion for the season, and Minnie would be without work until they returned again in the spring. Not everyone was affected by the Cone's departure for Baltimore. Many outdoor workers still had plenty to do and Arthur Moody made sure the large estate ran smoothly throughout the winter months. Minnie was a little sad that the summer was gone, and the Cones were leaving. She truly enjoyed her summer on the estate.

The Coffey family enjoyed Thanksgiving, and with the Thanksgiving holiday behind them, they were soon excited about planning Christmas activities. Christmas was a special holiday in the Coffey home. Finding the perfect tree to decorate, cookies to bake and decorations to hang, everyone had their part to do.

However, on December 8, 1908, something happened that no one expected. Moses Cone became gravely ill while in Baltimore and was rushed to Johns Hopkins hospital where he later died of pulmonary edema. He was only fifty one years old.

24

When the Cone's year around employees arrived to work at the estate the morning after his death, Arthur Moody, gathered them together outside of the mansion and gave them the unfortunate news. Everyone was in shock, since Mr. Cone was young and seemed to be in good health. Naturally their first concern was for Mrs. Cone, but they had to wonder too, how it would affect their employment at the mansion. Would Bertha Cone sell the huge home and permanently move to the city? What did that mean for all the employees who relied on permanent wages? So many unanswered questions, but for now, a time to mourn the passing of a good man.

Tilden got in his buckboard and quickly raced to Gilliam's farm to share the horrible news with Minnie. Before long, he was returning to the manor with Minnie. She wanted to be with her co-workers as they all attempted to process the sad news. Once Mr. Moody completed his meeting and everyone was about to go on with their business, Minnie and Tilden entered the mansion through the servant's entrance in back. They made their way to the mansion's kitchen where Minnie started a fire in the kitchen's stove and made a fresh pot of tea. She and Tilden sat at the big table, the very table Mr. and Mrs. Cone sat at every summer morning to have their breakfast. They shared stories of the Cones and life working at the mansion. Occasionally an employee or two, feeling the need to express their grief, would wander in out of the cold and pour a cup of tea. They would share with Minnie and Tilden their own stories of life with Mr. and Mrs. Cone and convey their sorrow. It was obvious that Mr. Cone was well thought of, and their sadness was genuine.

"Live your life to its fullest. You just never know when it will be your time to go," Tilden said. "We all believe we are too healthy or too young, or just too ornery to die, but it's simply just not true."

Minnie shook her head in disbelief. "I just can't believe this has happened. I am just stunned. What will Bertha do without him?"

"She has her sisters in Baltimore, so she has their support for now." Tilden was suddenly quiet, and obviously deep in thought. "We all have to wonder how secure our jobs are for now. I know it's not the appropriate time to be thinking of ourselves, but I wouldn't be human if it didn't cross my mind."

"Yes, I know, Uncle Tilden. No need to apologize, I understand. I suppose we will know soon enough what the future holds for us all, especially the full time employees."

Moses Herman Cone was buried near his beloved Flat Top Manor, facing east with an overview of the valley. After the funeral, Bertha Cone returned to Baltimore to live with her sister, Sophie for the remainder of that winter. The loyal staff cared for the great mansion and its animals as usual, with hope that Mrs. Cone would return in the spring.

It was soon Christmas, but for Minnie, something was missing from the celebration that year. Perhaps her heart was sad for Mrs. Cone, or perhaps her heart was a little sad due to the strained relationship she had with Jake. Minnie's mama sensed that Minnie was bothered and distracted. She tried to keep her occupied with various festivities of the season. They baked twice as many cookies as usual that Christmas. Minnie wondered what they would do with all those cookies, but Sarah Jane was determined to keep her mind and her hands busy all winter.

When Minnie's sister and Aunt Callie visited on Saturdays, the colorful quilts they had been laboring over were rolled out and strapped in the quilting frames. Occasionally Laura Moody sat in and helped with the quilting. The ladies continued the tidiest process of sewing each pattern and every block until the quilts were completed. Sarah Jane enjoyed working on the quilts, but also enjoyed entertaining Matt's little ones and stuffing them full of homemade sugar filled goodies. The quilts were truly stunning. They appreciated that the gorgeous hand stitched beauties were more than just a colorful piece of art, they were a necessity and would be much appreciated in the cold months still ahead.

Minnie admired her mother's strength. Minnie felt safe with her mama around. Sarah Jane was so confident and sure of herself and a no nonsense kind of lady, but very loving and nurturing. She was the youngest of seven children born to Joseph and Betty Barnes Isenhower in January of 1854 in Catawba County, North Carolina. Her ancestors emigrated from the Rhineland region in central Europe and were of German and Dutch descent. She married Gilliam Wyatt Coffey in 1875 and together they had eight children, Candus Luellen, Julia Sibbie, William Larkin, Etta Cordelia, Martha Jane, Joseph Monroe, Minnie Lee and Ethel M. Coffey.

Minnie and her brother, Joe, were the only children still at home. Minnie knew how much her mama missed Candus, Cordie and Julie and how much happier she would be having all her family close. Minnie also knew that her papa would do most anything to please her mama. So, she was curious what the future would bring for their family.

Twenty year old Joe was a very bright but shy and quiet man. He took life a bit more seriously than his brother and was often teased for it by Larkin. Joe reckoned staying in Blowing Rock was the reasonable thing to do, and Larkin was much more inclined to go along with the rest of the family and move, if that was the conclusion his parents thought best. Larkin was always open to new ideas and willing to try new things, where as Joe was content with the familiar and hesitated to change the way things were without good reason. He had a love for animals, and owned three beloved hound dogs that he raised from pups.

By March, Arthur Moody received word from Bertha Cone that she would be returning to the manor in April to spend the summer months with her sisters, Sophie and Clementine. Minnie was happy that Mrs. Cone would be coming home for the summer, but was sad knowing Mr. Cone would not be with her this time. In fact, he was already there buried on his beloved grounds two miles from the manor. Minnie had tolerated Mrs. Cone's sisters during their visits in the past. However, now they were a poor substitute for the man himself, and she would have the extra mouths to feed and please as well. The sisters could be obnoxious at times, not to mention demanding. It was no wonder to Minnie that neither had husbands. The staff was always relieved when the sisters went home to Baltimore after their visits with the Cones. It would be a long season with the both of them there at the manor all summer long.

Despite having the Lindau sisters to contend with, Minnie looked forward to going back to work and seeing Bertha Cone and the staff. She also looked forward to the warmer weather and her walks on the grounds of the beautiful estate. Her thoughts were often with Mrs. Cone, in hopes she was adjusting to life after her husband's untimely demise.

Spring of April, 1909 soon arrived and life at Flat Top Manor seemed to burst with activity. Anticipating the Cone's return was always a busy and special time of the year. Spring was a time of rebirth, everything old was new again. It was nice seeing new faces and familiar faces as well. It would not be the same without the most familiar face of all, however. Mr. Cone would be missed, there was no doubt about it. None the less, everyone was clear on the role they played to keep the grand estate up and running as efficiently as possible. Without Mr. Cone there to make a lot of the major decisions, it was up to Mr. Moody to successfully manage the staff and the business of the manor.

Anticipating Mrs. Cone's arrival, Minnie got an early start in her kitchen. She cleaned and took inventory of supplies she would need to get started preparing meals for Mrs. Cone and her two sisters. She was happy to be back at the manor, but would miss Mama and Papa too. Even though she saw them most every weekend, it was still a little sad to move out of her familiar and loving surroundings for the summer months.

It was not long before Minnie welcomed a visit by Uncle Tilden. He got her attention by tapping on the back kitchen window, and waving to her through the glass. He quickly made his way into the kitchen to say hello.

"Do you believe we're back working again, Minnie?" Tilden said with a smile. "Where did the winter months go?"

"It was a sad winter, Uncle Tilden." Minnie's tone took a very serious turn. "This place has an odd feel to it, don't you think? Like something's just not right, it's just so unsettling."

Tilden's smile faded and he became suddenly curious about Minnie's concerns. He slowly walked around the room, with fists on hips looking at the walls, table and kitchen area.

"I don't get it, what am I missing? What am I suppose to feel?" he finally replied.

"I don't know, Uncle Tilden. Just an eerie feeling, like Mr. Cone is still here. I'm not saying I believe in ghosts, and I don't want to sound loony. I am just saying his presence is still here."

"Moses Cone was bigger than life, but he's not coming back. He was a powerful man, but I wouldn't go as far as to think he could come back from the dead. I am sure his presence is felt in a lot of places, Minnie. He's here because you want him to be here. He will be sorely missed by a lot of people, and he will always be a big part of this place."

"I don't like change, and I reckon I'm just not use to people dying. As you well know, my baby sister, Ethel died when I was four. When she cried I would rock her to sleep for Mama. That's how I remember her, in my arms. I've been very fortunate in my life. Nobody else I know has died."

"Life goes on, Minnie. We miss those who have departed, but we got to keep living and doing the best we can," Tilden encouraged her. "Speaking of the living, Mrs. Cone will be here soon. I'd better get going."

Bertha Cone and her sisters arrived later that afternoon. She greeted the staff and the three women retired to their rooms until the dinner hour.

During dinner, Minnie noticed how depressed and gaunt Mrs. Cone seemed. She was very quiet, and the sparkle seemed lost from her brown eyes. It was heartbreaking and unnerving to see the transformation Bertha took from extraordinarily happy to incredibly sad. Under normal circumstances, Bertha's sisters would have been comical as they seemed to talk nonstop through dinner. The constant chatter reminded Minnie of the chickens in the hen house out back, but Bertha hardly said a word as she slowly sipped her soup. Once or twice she made eye contact with Minnie as she served their meal and attempted a smile to be friendly. Minnie felt the need to go to her and comfort her with a hug, but she knew that would be highly inappropriate. Minnie knew life at Flat Top Manor would never be the same again.

The summer went by slowly and the energy level that Mr. Cone usually brought to the manor was obviously missing for everyone working there. Life was just not the same without the man whose vision was to make the estate a grand and beautiful working summer home.

31

Minnie often visited with Mrs. Cone, when time permitted, but conversing with her became very difficult. Small talk was out of the question as Mrs. Cone seemed to have problems concentrating. She pretty much kept to herself and her relationships with the employees were very distant. Minnie knew she did not intend to be rude, but needed time to heal. This was simply her way of dealing with grief. Still, for Minnie, it was sad knowing life at the manor would be forever changed.

4 Candus Returns Home

The year 1909 brought with it more grandchildren for Sarah Jane and Gilliam. Matt and Hoyt brought little George into the world. Julia and Walter had a daughter, Tessie, in Washington State.

The summer of 1910 was strangely uneventful, but in the autumn after apple harvest, Candus and Lee made an unexpected visit. Their goal was to coax the family into returning with them to Washington State in the spring. They attempted to convince them moving was in their best interest. They promised the family a better and happier life in a land with more opportunities for them all. Candus vowed never to give up until the family agreed to move.

Candus and Lee did not bring Ruie with them on their visit to North Carolina. As she was seventeen now and nearly able to care for herself, they left her in the care of the Copple family back in Okanogan. The Copples were good friends of the family and they were sure she was in good hands. Ruie also had Cordie and Julie available to her if she needed something. Candus was very comfortable leaving her behind.

When Minnie said farewell to Mrs. Cone that October, she was fairly certain it would be the last season she would cook for her, and even more sadly, probably the last time she would ever see Bertha Cone again. It was particularly difficult to leave Bertha, knowing how sad and unsettled she was. The timing was all wrong and Minnie felt incredibly guilty. Minnie knew that Arthur would find her another cook, however, and the manor would go on working just fine without her. In time, Bertha Cone would adjust and her life would go on. Minnie knew she had to go on with her own life as well.

By the winter of 1910, the family was seriously considering the move west. Candus was very stubborn and very persuasive. Her persistence finally paid off and the family committed to the move. Minnie's work at the manor was indeed done and she realized once she made the move west, she would most likely never return to Blowing Rock again.

Sarah Jane was happy to have Candus and Lee home for the holidays that winter, however, she was a little sad her daughters Cordie and Julia were not there. The sisters were home with their families and of course, Ruie, was staying with the Copple family. One day, she hoped they would all be together for the holidays.

The joyous Christmas of 1910 quickly turned tragic when Candus and Lee got word that Ruie had been stricken with illness and had passed away on Christmas Eve. Her death was a bit of a mystery. They believed the poor girl died of sepsis. Candus was very sad that she had not been there for Ruie when she became so ill, but was comforted to know her sisters were there to care for her. Unfortunately, Candus and Lee were not able to travel home due to the frigid weather, and could not make the arrangements or attend Ruie's funeral. Candus felt sad and somewhat frustrated she was so removed from the process. However, there was just no way possible for her to return home in the middle of winter. Ruie was buried at the Okanogan Cemetery in the family plot.

Once the shock of losing Ruie was not so heavy in their hearts, it was time to continue the plans and preparations for the move. The objective was to move west by the end of March. Gilliam quickly found buyers for his farm and started making arrangements with his family for the big move. Candus and Lee took charge of the most important arrangements of all. They chartered the train west and arranged for the steam boat to haul them and their belongings up the Columbia River once they reached Wenatchee, Washington.

Much to Gilliam's surprise, friends and neighbors from Watauga County, expressed an interest in joining them. It would seem hard times called for extreme measures for some. In all, reservations were made for six families, a total of thirty people leaving Watauga County. Accommodations were made for adequate numbers of baggage cars to hold all of the possessions thirty people could move, including Joe's three beloved hound dogs.

One of the extra passengers would be a friend of Joe Coffey. His name was Charles Martin Harrell. He had been in the army, last serving at Fort McDowell, California in the 19th infantry, "M" Company and had decided not to re-enlist after his discharge in December, 1910.

During the Spanish-American War, the 19th was one of the first units dispatched. Transported by train to Mobile and then Tampa, on July 21st the regiment boarded the USS Florida and USS Cherokee to set sail for what was then called Porto Rico. They spent a year in Ponce performing guard and provost duty, then sailed to New York where they boarded trains to the west coast. On July 27, 1899 they sailed for Manila.

The regiment was broken into company-sized units and participated in many battles with the insurgents before returning to the U.S. in 1902. They served a second tour in the Philippines from 1905 to 1907 and a third and final tour from February 1910 to May of 1912. Charles served from June 1908 until December 1910, active duty toward the end of the war.

He was in need of a fresh start and thought a new beginning in a new state could be just what he needed. With very little coaxing from Joe, Charlie agreed to leave his parents behind and ride the train west from Watauga County.

Matt and Hoyt welcomed a new daughter, Zola May Cook into the world during this very hectic time planning their trip west. Matt took a break from her packing after the baby was born, but it was not long until she was back at work packing and making her own arrangements.

Larkin and Emma had the furthest to travel, since they were thirty miles from Gilliam and Sarah Jane's farm. Once the sale of their farm went through, they immediately prepared for the journey. In March, they sold what they could not take with them and started packing their wagon for the trip to Blowing Rock to meet up with his folks. It would not be easy traveling with two year old baby Ethel. The trip would take four days, with their team of slow oxen pulling them and their heavy wagon carrying what was left of their possessions. Once they arrived at Gilliam and Sarah Jane's home, they would rest awhile before proceeding on with the family by horse and wagon to the train station twenty miles away in Elk Park, North Carolina.

With Candus's help, Minnie stayed very busy helping her mama and papa pack their belongings. The work was often interrupted when a bit of nostalgia got the best of her. If she came across a toy, memento or a trinket from her childhood, she would have to pause to pay homage and reflect on what a wonderful life she had in the only house she had ever called home. Of course, the mansion was her home for three months out of the year, but she knew that old farm house would always truly be home for her.

Much of the furniture was given away, some of it going to Tilden and Callie and some of it left behind for the new home owners. They packed the smaller items that were easier to haul and transfer from the wagons to the train.

After church that Sunday, Minnie broke the unavoidable news to Jake. He seemed to take it well, but it was no great surprise to him. He knew it was only a matter of time before they announced their big move west. Jake and Minnie parted as friends, and vowed to keep in touch with letters. Minnie knew that Jake would never keep such a promise to write. Once the family left Blowing Rock, she knew all ties with Jake would be severed forever.

Minnie tried to spend as much time as possible with Uncle Tilden and Aunt Callie. They would be the people she would miss the most, and it was very sad to think of leaving them behind, not knowing if she would ever see them again. Despite the fact that Sarah Jane was in favor of the move, she knew it would be very difficult to leave her brother, Tilden behind. They had always been close, although Tilden was considerably younger. Sarah Jane knew the move would not be without regret.

The end of the month quickly arrived, and all the planning was now coming together. It was all so surreal for Minnie. It was one thing to consider moving, it was quite another to realize it was actually happening.

Larkin, Emma and two year old Ethel arrived at the family farm after a long difficult four days journey. Soon, they would be pressing on to Elk Park with the family. In those few days, there would be little rest, however. There was still much to do and there would be no rest for any of them until they were safely on the train headed west. Only then would they have time to sit, relax and consider their future.

Fortunately, the weather cooperated with them. It turned out to be a sunny and pleasant spring which made all the hard work more bearable. Minnie took a much needed break on the front porch steps with her guitar. The sun warmed her face and calmed her soul as she strummed her old guitar. It was a relaxing pause from all the hard work preparing the wagons for the twenty mile haul to the train station.

They were on a deadline to catch the train in Elk Park and make their transfer in Johnson City, Tennessee with the train going west. The pressure was on and tensions were high. Keeping their schedule mixed with emotions over leaving their home made for a sometimes stressful atmosphere. Minnie enjoyed being alone to relax and imagine how her future might be in Washington with her sisters.

Tilden, Callie and their children visited during this time to lend a hand. John and Laura Moody also helped with the packing and brought a picnic lunch to share with the family. Minnie looked forward to their visits, and it was always a good excuse to take a break from the packing and cleaning when they showed up. Minnie cherished every second with them all, knowing soon the opportunity to be with them would be lost, perhaps forever.

The night before their journey began Minnie sat on mama's rocking chair, which had been left on the porch for the new owners. It was a warm clear spring night. She slowly rocked and stared at the stars through the ivy that draped over the front porch, trying to enjoy her very last night in Blowing Rock. She wanted to take it all in so she could remember her last perfect night there at home in the mountains of North Carolina. The smell of the magnolia tree in bloom, the sound of the whippoorwills, the red wolves howling in the distance, she appreciated it all that night. Minnie anticipated another deep breath of fresh mountain air but quickly started to cough and gag. She jumped to her feet screaming and made a run for the front door.

"Oh my goodness!" she screamed as she slapped her hand over her mouth.

Before Minnie could get to the door, Gilliam quickly opened the door and Larkin ran outside to rescue Minnie. As soon as Larkin's foot hit the front porch, he knew what Minnie was screaming about. The stench of skunk quickly filled the air. Gilliam quickly slammed the door shut from inside the house once he recognized the foul odor, leaving Minnie and Larkin standing on the front porch gagging. Gilliam, being in an impish mood that evening, put his foot in front of the door, blocking their entrance.

"Papa! You open this door! You ornery old coot!" Larkin yelled while pushing on the door with his shoulder. He tried not to breathe in the odor that was getting worse by the second but that was not easy to do with all the yelling he was doing. Gilliam took mercy and removed his foot. Larkin and Minnie quickly stumbled into the house, slamming the door behind them.

"What's the matter with you, Papa? Are you crazy? Larkin screeched.

"Papa that was mean!" Minnie yelled as she started to giggle. She put her arm around her papa and hugged him.

"Pee yew, Minnie Lee, you stink!" Gilliam teased.

Minnie pushed him away and slapped him on the shoulder. "Stop it, now you behave!" she replied with a grin.

"Well y'all certainly know how to make our last night in this house a memorable one!" Sarah Jane teased. "I certainly hope those hounds don't find that skunk or they aren't going anywhere with me tomorrow."

Candus, Lee and Joe all had a good laugh at their expense. Matt was also enjoying a good laugh, when all of a sudden her laughter turned to tears. Sarah Jane hurried to comfort her.

"What's wrong, Matt? What is it child?" Sarah Jane asked.

"I love it here, Mama. I will miss this place, skunks and all. It's so sad to leave it all behind," Matt answered through her tears.

While trying to hold back her own tears, Minnie put her arms around her mama and sister. "It will be alright, Matt. Please don't be sad," Minnie reassured her. "It's not where you live so much, it's about having our family with us that makes us happy."

Martha's husband, Hoyt stood watching the women huddled together crying.

"Now you're telling me you don't want to move, Matt? Now's not the time to say you don't want to move, not when we're packed and about to leave!" Hoyt yelled with obvious frustration in his voice.

Annoyed with his son-in-law, Gilliam gave Hoyt the look of condemnation only a father could give. Hoyt never said another word. He quietly sat down at the only table left inside the house and shuffled his playing cards. Card playing was considered sinful to Sarah Jane and Gilliam and not allowed in their home, shuffling cards did not help Hoyt's cause at all, but Gilliam chose not to waste his time with Hoyt any longer that night.

5 Saying Goodbye

The day had finally arrived. Minnie dreaded saying goodbye to Aunt Callie and Uncle Tilden. When all the wagons carrying the family and their belongings pulled away from the farm, Tilden and Callie were standing there waving goodbye. Attempting to wave back to them, Minnie's emotions got the best of her and she broke down and began to cry. Sarah Jane, also upset by leaving her brother and her home behind, put her arm around Minnie to console her.

The twenty mile journey to Elk Park had begun. Minnie was anxious to board the train just so she had a more comfortable seat in which to sit, and be able to doze off and nap without fear of falling out of a wagon. The ride was bumpy and dusty and at times she felt nauseous and unwell.

Gilliam had arranged for Mr. Baxter, the livery stable owner to purchase the wagons and horses from his family once they unloaded their belongings and boarded the train in Elk Park. The other Watauga County passengers making the journey west with them would have to make their own arrangements.

When the Coffey family arrived at the Elk Park station, the train was already there and would be departing in three hours. This gave them little time to transfer everything from their wagons, including Joe's hound dogs, over to the train's baggage cars. They met up with the rest of the Watauga County passengers and made sure everyone was present and accounted for.

Once the baggage cars were loaded, the families boarded the East Tennessee and Western North Carolina Railroad train known by the locals as Tweetsie for its peculiar whistle. Their first stop would be Johnson City, Tennessee. There they would transfer all their belongings to a Burlington train that would head west by way of Kansas City, Missouri. This train would take them to Wenatchee, Washington where they would transfer their belongings to a steam boat that would take them up the Columbia River north to the small town of Brewster, Washington.

Joe found his friend, Charlie Harrell and offered help getting his few belongings on the train. Charlie was a pleasant looking squared jawed man with black wavy hair, crystal blue eyes and stood five foot six inches tall. He was a quiet but pleasantly charming man of twenty eight years old. Charlie was eager for an adventure and willing to experience a new way of life in a state so unlike his home of North Carolina. His parents, Jessie Harrell and Alidia Townsend Harrell tearfully said goodbye to their son, giving him one last hug before he boarded the train. .

When Minnie found her seat on the train, she quickly flopped down and sighed with relief. Finally, she could rest comfortably until they reached Johnson City. Holding her newborn baby, Matt sat down next to her and squeezed Minnie's hand with a smile. Her other three children shared a seat with husband, Hoyt. The rest of the family took their seats in front and behind the sisters. Joe sat next to Charlie a few rows away. Charlie waved to his parents from inside the train as it slowly pulled away from the station. It would be the last time he would ever see them again.

Minnie woke up from a sound sleep. The steady thumping of the train's metal wheels against the iron rail tracks had lulled her to sleep. Matt was fast asleep, her head rested on Minnie's shoulder while infant baby Zola May slept on her chest. The sun was blinding coming through the windows. Without disturbing her sister and the baby, Minnie rubbed her eyes and looked around the train car for her family. Mama and Papa were also sleeping and the rest of her family were quietly watching the scenery go by as the train chugged steadily down the tracks headed for Tennessee. Being old hands at this train travel business, Candace and Lee were both content reading a newspaper.

Minnie could see the back of Joe's head and could tell he was busy conversing with his friend, Charlie. She had never met Charlie, and Joe failed to introduce him to the family when he boarded the train in Elk Park. He did not go unnoticed, however. Minnie thought he was handsome, and she was curious to know who he was and how Joe knew him.

Sarah Jane brought along with her a large picnic basket full of sandwiches, cookies and various other good things to eat. However, with all the people to feed, the basket full of food would not last long. Eventually, someone would have to get off the train to buy food when it stopped for maintenance and water. There were also restaurants along the way that catered to train passengers.

Besides the humans who needed to eat, Joe's hounds were also hungry. There was access to the baggage car at the back of the train, so Joe was able to feed the dogs and look after them while the train was moving.

Taking advantage of one of Joe's doggie welfare visits, Minnie stopped him as he and Charlie passed on their way to the baggage car.

"Kiss the hounds on the noses for me," Minnie said grinning.

"I think they'd prefer a sandwich," Joe replied.

It was obvious to Joe that Minnie was looking past him, her eyes were on Charlie. Finally, it dawned on Joe to introduce them.

"Oh, I guess I never introduced you to Charlie. Minnie, this is my friend, Charlie Harrell. Charles, this is my little sister Minnie," Joe said as he stepped aside so Charlie could better see her.

Charlie reached his hand out to take hers. She quickly obliged to offer up a handshake. Charlie held her hand and was so mesmerized, he neglected to let go.

"So nice to meet you, Minnie," Charlie smiled.

"It's so good to meet you as well, but I think I might be having a sandwich soon, and I'll be needing that hand back," she joked.

Charlie quickly let go. "I'm so sorry, it's been a long day. I'm exhausted and not thinking straight. It was nice to meet you, Minnie."

"We're going back to check on the hounds now, you two can visit more later on. Lord knows there will be plenty of time for y'all to visit on this adventure," Joe moaned as he proceeded out the back of the train. Charlie followed him out, stopping to take one last glance Minnie's way before exiting through the door.

"That boy likes you, Minnie Lee," Matt teased.

"Nah, he's just being nice," Minnie replied.

"No, I think he really likes you. He's kind of short, but he has gorgeous blue eyes. I think he's kinda cute. At least you'll have someone interesting to talk to on this long train ride," Matt replied. "I should probably go sit with Hoyt. He's probably already upset with me for not sitting with him and the girls."

Minnie looked over the back of her seat to better see where Hoyt was seated. He was sitting in the seat behind her holding his young son, George. His head was laid back resting on the window and his mouth was wide open. A bit of drool was starting to form in the corner of his lips and strange wheezing noises were coming from his throat. His two little girls, Grace and Velma were piled against him sleeping soundly.

"Yep, he's really upset, Matt. He's back there chomping at the bit waiting for you," Minnie giggled. "Good thing those youngin's of yours like to sleep so much."

The two days ride seemed to go by quickly and soon the train was slowly pulling into the station at Johnson City, Missouri. Joe had traded seats with Minnie and she visited with Charlie most of the way there. Minnie thought he was a very charming man and wanted to get to know him better. She looked forward to visiting with him more on the remainder of the trip.

There was no time to be idle. As soon as the train came to a stop, the families were hurrying to gather their belongings as they began transferring property from one baggage car to the next. The porter confirmed their reservations before they were allowed to transfer their belongings to the newer bigger train headed west. Minnie and the family were excited about the new Pullman sleepers in the next train. The long trip would be much more bearable if they could sleep comfortably.

The belongings were transferred over to the west bound train with time to spare so the family gathered in a small café inside the train depot for a meal. Joe invited Charlie Harrell to join them, much to Minnie's delight. After their meal, they boarded the train and anticipated its departure from the station.

All was progressing as expected until they hit a snag in Kansas City. Their train car, including the luggage cars were switched to a side track for an entire day. This was a common occurrence for scheduling reasons, but they were disappointed they had lost an entire day in the process. By early morning the next day, they were on their way again.

Minnie and Charlie visited for hours and watched the beautiful scenery quickly pass by their window. Minnie was in awe of the countryside. She had never been west of North Carolina before and was amazed with the varieties of terrain and landscapes she was seeing on this journey. Having Charlie to visit with certainly made the long cross country trip go by quickly. The luxury of the Pullman train car made her appreciate much more the sacrifices others before her had endured when they settled the west by horse pulled wagons many years before. The west was definitely still the land of opportunity for anyone seeking a plot of land and the American dream. Candus and Lee did quite well with their farm and orchard. There was no reason why Gilliam and the rest of the family could not be as fortunate.

6 The Long Train Ride

Finally, they were far enough west, it felt like they were making progress. The train stopped in Billings, Montana for a quick lay over that morning and it was once again Lee's turn to buy food for the family. This time, he would be more attentive of his pocket watch and know how much time he had before returning to the train. On a previous stop, it could have been quite the predicament for the family when Lee got off the train to buy food and neglected to keep track of the time. He was one step away from missing the train that day. Candus scolded him for raising her blood pressure, and he promised to never let it happen again.

Larkin and Emma's baby, Ethel was doing well for a two year old. She was a good baby, and managed well during their week of travel. All five of the grandchildren spent a lot of time on Grandma Sarah Jane's lap. The other family members were happy to look out for the little ones too, giving their parents a chance to rest when they needed a break. Changing diapers were a little tricky, and absolutely the worst part about traveling with babies.

Walking around on the train was permitted, and everyone moved around as often as possible to stretch their legs and fight off boredom. Sometimes they would gather to have a snack together and visit. One day, the siblings were gathered around Charlie telling stories of their childhood and remembering funny anecdotes of their lives in Blowing Rock.

"Let me tell you something Joe and me did to our crazy neighbor back when we were teenagers," Larkin said to Charlie. "We discovered our nutty neighbor, Bob Johnson was coming over to our property nearly every morning. He'd come over and sit on the top of our grape arbor and take a poop."

"That's disgusting!" Charlie responded with a laugh.

"Yeah, but Larkin and I fixed him good," Joe replied.

"One morning before one of his visits, Joe and I went out to the grape arbor where he had been doing his business. We took the handsaw with us and cut half way through the arbor on both sides so when Johnson sat down, the arbor would be too weak to hold his weight," Larkin explained. "We had to step around all the crap on the ground. It was pretty bad."

"Yeah, and then we hid behind the trees and watched. Sure enough, Bob Johnson showed up, pulled down his trousers and made himself at home on our grape arbor," Joe said with a laugh.

"It held him awhile, just long enough to do his business, and then it collapsed!" Larkin explained. "He fell butt first straight down into all that poop he'd been leaving there for days."

"So much for the grape arbor," Charlie laughed. "But it served him right."

"Yeah, and Bob Johnson never set foot on our property again," Joe replied.

It would not be long now, and they would be in the state of Washington. The journey would not end at the train station in

Wenatchee, however. The family would arrive in Wenatchee in the evening and transfer their belongings to the wagons that would take them to the boat landing. Passengers going north were asked to board the boat in the evening and sleep on the carpets on board. The elder members of the family, not wanting to sleep on the boat's hard floor, elected instead to stay in a hotel room. They would have to be at the landing by 5:00 AM when the boat headed north.

The stern-wheel steamer would take them and their possessions from Wenatchee up river to Brewster Landing. The boat only made the trip north on the Columbia River twice weekly. If they missed the boat, they would have a few days wait before the next opportunity to go north. Arrangements were made for Julie's husband, Walter Robbins, Cordie's husband, Walter Cook, Lee's brother, Bob Cook and Bob's son, Walter to be in Brewster waiting for them with four horse teams to take them all on to Okanogan. If they missed the boat, it would be difficult to get word to the men there was a delay in their rendezvous. They were already a day behind schedule because of the layover in Kansas City.

Lee and Candus had plans to host the families on their farm in Spring Coulee, just southwest of the town of Okanogan. Some would stay in the main house, some in a nearby guest house and others would live in small houses they had on their property for their orchard laborers until they could establish themselves and find property of their own. Candus was so sure they would return with her, she had already made all the necessary arrangements before she left for North Carolina. Soon, all of her planning would come together and she would have all her family together again.

Charlie Harrell made no arrangements past getting to the town of Okanogan. His intention was to find an affordable place to stay until he could find work. He was a handy man and a fairly skilled carpenter and mason. He was sure he could find employment somewhere. Meeting Minnie Coffey was not part of his plans, however. She was an unexpected pleasure that could very well change every plan he ever had about his future. Charlie always thought of himself as a reasonable care-free man and was somewhat surprised by his feelings for Minnie. He started thinking about his future with her and this was astounding to him. He had never fallen for any woman like he did for Minnie.

Minnie, likewise, was very smitten with Charlie. She too started imagining her future with Charlie by her side. She even imagined what their children might look like. Could he be the one, she wondered? The notion was so inconceivable for her to comprehend considering the short time they knew each other. Could she be so infatuated with a man she hardly knew? Time would tell, and it was in God's hands for now.

Minnie thought the last day seemed to be the longest of the entire trip. When she would take naps, or sleep at night, she would always trade seats with Joe or sit with another family member. As innocent as it might be, Sarah Jane thought it inappropriate for Minnie and Charlie to sleep together in any capacity regardless that they were fully clothed and sitting upright.

Minnie could now see the sun starting to peak over the snow capped mountain top. This would be their last sunrise aboard the train. They had come a long way since North Carolina and they were making evident progress now. She could hardly wait to get off the train that evening and get onto that steamboat that would head north up the mighty Columbia River into Okanogan County.

Known simply as "the Okanogan", the county was the largest by land mass located in the north central part of Washington State. The vast Okanogan Valley stretched north well into British Columbia, Canada. The valley was a land of hundreds of lakes, rivers and streams. It was remote and rural but was once busy with many prospectors enroute to find riches in the gold fields of British Columbia. The valley had a rich history of famous Indians, fur trappers, farmers, ranchers, miners and railroad men wanting to tame the wild west. The word Okanogan is an Indian word meaning rendezvous. The first American Post was Fort Okanogan built in 1811 by the Astor's Pacific Fur Company. In 1859 the county experienced a gold rush when gold was discovered on the Similkameen River near Nighthawk.

The steam boat that would take the family north to Brewster was named The North Star. She was a ninety nine and a half foot stern wheel propulsion wooden hull boat built in 1902 by the Columbia and Okanogan Steam Navigation Company of Wenatchee. The twin steam engines were one hundred thirty horsepower. The boat had suffered damage in September of 1902 in the Entiat Rapids, but was rebuilt and put back into service in 1907. Normally, the North Star traveled as far north as Okanogan, but it was too early in the spring and the river was not high enough to make the trip that far north. Once the snow in the mountains melted and the river was high, the boat would then make the run north as far as the town of Okanogan. From past experience, Lee and Candus knew it would take about twelve hours to make the boat trip up river to Brewster. So far, they seemed to be pretty much on schedule.

When the train finally pulled into the Wenatchee train station, all of their possessions, including Joe's beloved hounds, were promptly transferred to wagons. From there, Gilliam, Sarah Jane, Candus and Lee checked into a Wenatchee hotel and the rest of the family made their way with the belongings to the boat landing where the North Star was docked.

Minnie was very curious to see a paddle boat and was very anxious to arrive at the landing. She was sure floating quietly on the river would be more pleasurable than listening to the constant thumping of the train tracks. She looked forward to the peace and quiet as she took in the beautiful landscapes, the big clear river, and all the natural wonders of the waterway. Minnie was told of the huge salmon and sturgeon in the river and she hoped to catch a glimpse of one jumping out of the water, or perhaps a fisherman landing a great prize. She was also excited to see the birds that were not native to North Carolina. Although eagles were not uncommon in her neck of the woods back in North Carolina, she was excited to see the large eagles that nested along the banks of the Columbia. Minnie wanted to enjoy every moment of her time on the river. Spending the twelve hours on the boat with Charlie was also very appealing. Sharing this journey with him was special and she loved every second of it.

When the wagons pulled into the landing known as the Wenatchee Reach, Minnie's eyes opened wide. Although dark, there was a full moon that seemed to light up the riverboat like a beacon in the night. There she sat, the paddle boat that would take them one step closer to home. The boat was a large double decked beauty. She could not wait to step on board and start up the river early the next morning. It took awhile to transfer all the people, belongings and hounds over to the boat, but once it was done, the families relaxed and tried to get some sleep on the hard floor of the boat before they headed north.

The next morning, Sarah Jane, Gilliam, Candus and Lee made it to the boat in plenty of time. They were not about to let the boat go without them. Minnie stood on the bow of the boat with Charlie and her family as the boat slowly pulled away from the landing. The paddle wheel started to churn and the adventure on the big river was about to begin. Once the sun came up, Minnie was able to admire the view as the boat proceeded up river. She was enchanted by the beautiful river, the scenery and the entire experience. This country was so different from where she came, but very beautiful in a different kind of way. She could see the snow capped Cascade Mountain range in the distance and on both sides of the river rolling green hills of spring grasses, a brown sandy shoreline, sage brush, yellow balsamroot and various wildflowers in bloom. She could smell the sweet apple blossoms from a nearby orchard in full bloom. This new world was alive with spring.

Minnie turned to a crew member, "where are all the evergreens?" she asked. "I heard the trees were very large in the west."

"In the mountains," he answered. "The higher up you go, the more trees you'll find. Yes, ma'am we have some pretty big trees, I'd say."

"Does it rain here much?" she asked him.

"It rains, but I think you are confusing our area of the state with the west side. It rains a lot and it's pretty green over there, this here is dry like the desert," he explained.

"I've never heard of growing apples in the desert," she said to Charlie.

"Apparently so. Your brother-in-law grows apples too, Minnie,"

"Why, yes indeed, they do grow apples in the desert. How interesting," Minnie replied. "But then again, look at all this water to irrigate with."

"You're enjoying this, aren't you?" Charlie asked with a smile.

"Yes I am, I am learning so much. I wonder what it will be like where we live?" Minnie wondered aloud.

"It won't be long now, and you'll know," Charlie replied.

"I can't wait to get home," Minnie said with a sigh. "Charlie, I wonder if they have skunks in Okanogan?"

7 Boat Ride Up the Columbia

The paddle boat was not as quiet as Minnie imagined it would be. However, she did not mind the steady soft thumping of the forceful wooden wheel churning round and round pushing the mighty boat up stream. With every turn, she was closer to her new home.

The family and others relaxed in the passenger quarters of the boat as it made its way north. Being on the river made the temperatures cooler and by late afternoon, everyone was wearing jackets and sweaters as they approached the Entiat Rapids. Winches had to be fastened to boulders on the bank to pull them through the rapids. This was a very dangerous point in the river, and had nearly destroyed The North Star in a previous attempt up the river in 1902. Everyone on board was very nervous until the boat managed its way through the rapids without incident.

When the boat passed the town of Pateros, the family knew they were very close to the end of the boat ride. Brewster Landing was now only six miles away. Their anticipation and excitement grew with every turn of the boat's paddle wheel. It had been a long exhausting journey west but the end was near. In a few days, the entire family would be together again. As much as Minnie enjoyed the boat ride, she was ready for it to end. Sarah Jane and Gilliam were very anxious to see their daughters again. Julie and Cordie were waiting for them in Spring Coulee, but their husbands would be at the landing when the family arrived in Brewster.

The horse and wagon ride to Spring Coulee would take all day. After a twelve hour boat ride, there would not be enough hours in the day to continue on. Besides the fact that everyone was already exhausted, no one wanted to travel at night. They would stay in a hotel, and then proceed on to Spring Coulee first thing the next morning. It would be the last leg of this incredible journey. Once again, they would transfer all their belongings, including Joe's hounds, from the boat to the wagons waiting for them in Brewster.

As the boat slowly pulled into the landing, the family spotted Walter Robbins, Walter Cook, Bob Cook, and Bob's son waiting for them with four teams of horses. They waved and yelled hello to the men. Larkin gave out a loud whistle to get their attention. At last, thirty passengers, made up of family and friends from North Carolina had arrived in Brewster, Washington.

By the time the families arrived at the Gamble Hotel, Minnie was totally exhausted. It had been a long day, and she had not slept well the previous night. After having dinner with her family at a local restaurant, she was in a hurry to check in to her room at the hotel and take a nice hot leisurely bath. After her bath, Minnie quickly crawled into the warm comfortable feather bed and snuggled up in the soft quilts. Her thoughts turned to Blowing Rock, her Aunt Callie and Uncle Tilden. She wondered if the people who bought their farm liked living there. She wondered how Bertha Cone was getting along with her new cook and she wondered if Jake missed her yet.

The brilliant sunshine coming through the window woke Minnie the next morning. She could not believe it was already morning, it seemed she had just shut her eyes. Her body was tired and she did not think she was capable of crawling out of that wonderful bed. Minnie worried about her folks. She knew if she was tired, Sarah Jane and Gilliam were spent. It would not be long now, and they could all rest in Spring Coulee.

Matt burst through the door and jumped up on Minnie's bed.

"Are you ready to end this journey, little sister of mine?" she cheerfully asked.

"Why are you so happy? You're just too happy, no one should be so happy in the morning," Minnie replied as she curled up in her bedding and turned away from Matt. "I slept like a log, and I am still exhausted. Why aren't you exhausted? You have kids and a husband, you should be worn out."

"I'm too happy to be exhausted. I am excited to get out of this little town and get on the road. The sooner we get out of here, the sooner we'll be in Spring Coulee. I want this all to be over with, and I want to start living a normal life," Matt explained. "I'm tired of Hoyt being so tired and grumpy."

"Yeah, well Hoyt is always unhappy about something. I am ready for this journey to be over with too. I'd better get up and get dressed before Papa comes looking for me," Minnie said as she threw the covers back and got out of bed.

The family gathered their belongings, packed a lunch for the road and had breakfast before they started north on the final phase of their long odyssey. They left Brewster early, it would be an all day trip and they did not want to travel in darkness.

Finally, the wagons were rolling north. Minnie sat in the wagon with the hounds. She was amused by how they were getting along during their cross country adventure. They sat in the wagon with their long floppy ears and big noses staring at Minnie. She tossed them pieces of toast she saved from her morning breakfast. One dog was a master at playing catch. One dog seemed oblivious to the flying bread snacks and was uninterested in making the effort to catch any of them. The third hound made a valiant attempt at catch, but the bread bounced off the top of his head with most attempts.

The horse teams pulled the full wagons up over Brewster Flats and then down into the low land of the valley along the river. They made occasional stops to rest and water the horses along the Okanogan River. Minnie was happy to stretch her legs and inspect all the wildflowers along the hillside or throw a few rocks into the river. The ride was uncomfortable and she was anxious for the trip to end, but Minnie never complained. She felt if anyone had the right to complain, it was her Mama and Papa. They were older with aches and pains of their own, but they never were one to complain about much.

They stopped again in Malott, the first town they came to. It seemed to take forever to get there, but it was an obvious indication they were again making good progress. They had nine more miles to travel before reaching the town of Okanogan. After a brief rest, the wagons were rolling again.

Sarah Jane was a tough lady with a strong disposition, but even she was showing signs now of succumbing to fatigue and sheer exhaustion. Minnie worried about her and Gilliam both. Matt managed to hold on to infant Zola May while she slept, despite the bumpy uncomfortable wagon ride. Her little girls stayed curled up next to her. Hoyt sat up at Matt's side most of the trip attempting to stay awake but his head bobbed around and his chin kept bouncing off his chest. Charlie sat with Walter Robbins on the driver's bench. Larkin and his family were in one of the other wagons with Joe, and Candus and Lee were in yet another wagon.

All of the wagons were full of families with their possessions eager to start their new lives in a new land. Most were farmers, eager to find a piece of land to work, but getting settled first would take some time. Minnie thought it amazing how many people were willing to give up their homes, their families and everything familiar to them and start a new life in a strange new land they had not even visited up to this point. Here they all were, about to reach their destination, a small town thousands of miles away from the only place they had ever called home. The will of the human spirit was a powerful thing.

Minnie managed to doze off a few times but the bumpy rough road kept waking her. She turned to look ahead of the wagon and could see a town in the distance. She quickly set up on her knees to get a better look.

"Is that Okanogan, Walter?" she asked with excitement.

"Yes, Minnie, that would be the town of Okanogan, in the county of Okanogan. So what do you think of it so far?" Walter replied.

"It's beautiful!" Minnie proclaimed.

"She's just delirious from the long trip," Charlie joked.

Soon the wagons were in the heart of the town. Walter, in the lead wagon stopped his horses on the main street between The Hotel Okanogan and the livery stable.

"The town is smaller than I thought it would be, and sandy, it's really kind of desolate. Don't you agree, Charlie?" Minnie observed.

"After seven days on the road, any place looks like heaven. But I have to admit, this place is a little barren," he replied.

"Those staying in town need to unload their belongings. We'll be headed to Spring Coulee soon, so don't wander off," Walter announced to the travelers and then turned to Minnie. "Don't worry, Minnie. This little town is growing every day, we have four hotels now. Just look over there, we have ourselves a school now too," Walter said as he pointed up the hill. "There's apple orchards popping up everywhere too. This land is rich for growing crops."

Charlie helped Sarah Jane, Minnie, Matt and the children down from the wagon. They stretched their backs and walked around to get their legs working again.

Minnie looked around at everyone and started laughing. "Ya'll should see yourselves! You're covered in dust and dirt. All I can see are the whites of your eyes!"

"Well, you're none too clean yourself, girl," Matt replied with a giggle.

"So what's across the river?" Charlie asked Walter.

"Everything on the east bank of the Okanogan River is Colville Indian Reservation," Walter replied.

"Indians?" a surprised Sarah Jane asked.

"Yep, Indians!" Walter replied with a smile.

"Oh my!" Sarah Jane said putting her hand on her chest.

Gilliam slowly stepped down off the wagon. Minnie could tell he was very disenchanted with what he saw. The little town did not impress him, this was obvious.

"There's nothing to this town. The streets are just trails in the sage brush and rocks," Gilliam said in a disappointed tone. "Is there even a Baptist Church in this town?"

Being that Papa was not talking to anyone in particular, Minnie knew he was upset and not at all thrilled about what he was seeing before him.

"Not to worry, Gilliam. The town is growing. They're about to complete a major irrigation project. Soon, you'll grow all the crops you want!" Walter reassured. "All this will be green soon! And no, we have a Methodist and Presbyterian but no Baptist."

"I'm not a Methodist, nor a Presbyterian," Gilliam snarled. "I'll be needn' just the Baptist."

The families heard a very strange loud noise quickly approaching. They all turned to look as an automobile passed by. The driver honked his horn, startling Sarah Jane into dropping her picnic basket, and the driver waved as he passed the small crowd.

"Well, I never!" Sarah Jane yelped as she picked up her basket.

"Looky there!" Larkin yelled to his brother. "That's one beautiful automobile. I'm gonna have one of those someday, Joe."

"Just don't honk at Mama when you get one Lark, or she might beat ya with her picnic basket." Joe replied with a grin.

"That was Mr. Masters. He's with the railroad. Of course a railroad man can afford it, but he's not the only one in town with an automobile. It's the sign of the times, Lark. Everyone will have one before long," Walter said.

The families mingled together and visited, knowing this would be the end of the line for some of them leaving the group. Charlie would stay at the hotel in town that evening, and perhaps start looking for work the next day. After spending a week with Minnie, Charlie was accustom to being with her and was not ready to let her go.

Minnie approached Charlie to tell him goodbye for now. Charlie smiled at her and gently wiped away the dirt and grime from her face with his thumb.

"I know, I look awful," Minnie smiled.

"No, you look beautiful, as always," Charlie replied.

Charlie kissed her cheek and gave her a hug. "I'll see you soon, ya hear?"

"You'd better, Mr. Harrell. You best find me," she replied.

Minnie turned and walked away, joining her family back at Walter Robbins's wagon. They got back on the wagon to resume their journey to Spring Coulee. As the wagons pulled away, Minnie waved to Charlie. He stood there in the middle of the road, one fist on his hip and the other hand in the air waving back to her. She watched him until he was out of sight.

"This creek here is called Salmon Creek," Walter explained to the family as the wagon wheels kept turning. They followed the creek for about four miles until the road came to a Y. They took a left and continued for another couple miles until Walter pulled the horse team to the right and through the gates of a spacious farm.

"You're home, Minnie Lee!" Walter yelled to Minnie.

Minnie put her hand on Gilliam's shoulder for balance and stood up in the wagon. It was a beautiful place, indeed. Lee had a large orchard at the front of his house going out to the main road and south, and a large alfalfa pasture at the north end of his property. Lee had always bragged about his water well that easily accommodated his large orchard and hay crop. Minnie could see that his place was well taken care of and there was plenty of water. An abundance of water was not always so common in this area. As the wagons approached the house, she saw cattle, horses, pigs, chickens and rabbits. As soon as the wagon stopped, Minnie jumped down and ran to pet a curious horse that stood in his pen outside the barn area.

 Cordie and Julie ran out of the house to greet their family. Sarah Jane was so excited to see her daughters, she grabbed them tight and cried tears of joy. Suddenly, there seemed to be children ranging from ages two to fourteen coming from every corner of the farm. They appeared from the barn, from the chicken coop, from the orchard. Soon all eight grandkids were there to meet their grandparents, aunts, uncles and young cousins for the first time. Sarah Jane held out her arms in an attempt to take them all in to her bosom. Gilliam grabbed baby Ethel from Larkin's arms, and then grabbed up Matt's little girls in his arms and joined in the hug. Once again, the tears started to flow down Sarah Jane's cheeks. It was a splendid celebration and finally, she had all her children and grandchildren together. This was something she feared would never happen in her life time.

Gilliam was in better spirits after seeing his daughters and grandchildren, but Sarah Jane was already concerned that Gilliam would want to return to North Carolina. Time would tell. But for now, everyone was together as a family and this was home.

In the next days and weeks, the family started to feel a bit more settled. Charlie and Minnie continued to see one another and grew closer with each visit. With the town of Okanogan and surrounding communities growing so quickly, there always seemed to be plenty of work to do for the men folk. Charlie stayed busy working as a carpenter and handyman, and was feeling comfortable in his new surroundings.

The irrigation district project on Pogue Flat was completed providing more jobs for the area. Soon there was plenty of water in places that previously had very little water for growing anything. The Okanogan Irrigation Project was started in 1905 with the approval of the U.S. Department of the Interior, making it the first U.S. Bureau of Reclamation project in the state of Washington.

Okanogan County became a booming agricultural valley and various crops were sprouting up everywhere. Apple, pear and cherry orchards were popping up across the county, farms and ranches were thriving. The new town upriver called Omak was also flourishing during this busy time in the county's history.

By July of 1911, Minnie and Charlie had decided to be wed. Seeing how happy Charlie and Minnie were together, her family was very pleased to celebrate their union. On July 30, 1911, surrounded by family, Minnie Lee Coffey became Mrs. Charles Martin Harrell in a civil ceremony at the county courthouse in Conconully.

Charlie and Minnie lived in a modest home along Salmon Creek not far from Spring Coulee. She loved having a home of her own, and lived close enough to her family that she saw them often. Charlie stayed busy as a carpenter and they were happy. By the end of September, it was quite evident to Minnie that her family would be growing. She announced to Charlie she was with child. The doctor figured she was due late April or early May. The family was elated and started planning for the newest member of the Coffey-Harrell family.

Despite Gilliam's disappointment with the move, life was good, it would seem. However, Larkin's wife, Emma made it known she was not so happy with the move west either. Like Gilliam, she was disappointed once the family arrived in Okanogan. The rest of the families who had traveled so far to make a better life for themselves were doing well and seemed very content and happy.

Happiness turned to the deepest kind of sorrow in November. Cordie and Walter's four year old daughter, Hazel was tragically killed when she fell off a wagon and was accidentally run over by the wheel. Cordie's grief overcame her, she was inconsolable and very distant from everyone for months after Hazel's death.

Although Minnie really only knew Hazel for a short while, she had grown very fond of her beautiful little blonde haired niece. Hazel was a bright curious child full of life and wonder. Minnie had known the precious girl for only eight months before the tragedy that claimed her short lived life. As strong as Minnie's faith was, it certainly made her question God's reasons for allowing Hazel to die so tragically and so very young. She was heartbroken for Cordie. What could anyone possibly say or do to make the pain less for her sister? The love of her family guided Cordie through that awful period in her life and only time helped her deal with the pain. Little Hazel's sweet laugh would live on in their hearts.

8 A Baby For Minnie and Charlie

With the family still grieving for Hazel, their sadness turned to joy when Minnie and Charlie welcomed their first daughter into the world the following year. Leda Ruby Harrell was born April 26, 1912. Sarah Jane's baby now had a baby of her own. She hoped that having the grandchildren near would sway Gilliam into staying put, and give up the notion of eventually returning to North Carolina. Sarah Jane was thoroughly enjoying her children and her grandchildren. The thought of moving away from them, after everything they had been through to get everyone together was inconceivable.

Soon after Leda's arrival, Emma and Larkin welcomed a baby girl of their own, Edna Coffey on May 8. Also, Julie and Walter had twin daughters, Verlie and Verna Robbins that year and Cordie and Walter Cook had a daughter they named Gladys. The family was blessed again with healthy happy babies.

Unfortunately, just when the family seemed to be adjusting to the tragedy of Hazel's death, misfortune was again about to raise its ugly head. Hoyt announced to the family his intentions to move back to North Carolina. This was devastating news for the family. Matt was heartbroken, but felt she had no choice but to leave with her husband. She could not raise her babies alone without him. Matt prepared to return to her home state, but Hoyt made some last minute plans of his own that no one really understood, including a very upset Matt. They eventually settled in Hanover, Virginia. There, Matt gave birth to another daughter, Hazel, named after her niece who was tragically killed in 1906. Matt was sad that they did not return to North Carolina. She did not want to move at all, but if she had to go anywhere, she would prefer to go back to North Carolina. She did not know anyone in Virginia and would resent the move for the rest of her life.

When the Coffeys arrived in Okanogan, there was no Baptist church in the area. The Coffeys and Cooks, with a small group of citizens founded the first Baptist church congregation in Okanogan on September 8, 1912. Without a building to meet in, they would take turns having Sunday worship services in homes of the members. On December 7, 1912 the church members voted to raise money to purchase land from Frank Reed on which to construct their church building. The first Deacons of their church were Lee Cook and E.L. Bolin. The first Trustees were James Shull, E.L. Bolin and Walter Robbins. The church's first pastor was Elder W.J. Parmley. David and Lilly Townsend were also charter members of this church, to be known as the First Missionary Baptist Church.

Gilliam became ill the end of 1912 and was diagnosed with a heart condition known then as dropsy. By March of 1913, he was pretty much bed fast. Gilliam knew he was very sick and would never return to North Carolina. Sarah Jane was sad knowing her husband was never happy with their move to the northwest, but it was obvious at this point, they would never be returning to the Appalachian Mountains they once called home.

On May 22, 1913 the doctor called the family to Gilliam's bedside to say their goodbyes. With the exception of Matt, each of his children took their turn visiting their stricken father for the last time. Matt was heartbroken she could not be there to tell her Papa goodbye. When it was Minnie's turn with him, she stood by his bed and held his hand.

"Papa, its Minnie. I love you, Papa," Minnie said as she squeezed her father's hand.

Gilliam opened his tear filled eyes and looked at Minnie. "I love you, Minnie Lee," he responded with a labored whisper. "Take care of that little one for me, she's a beauty."

Minnie spent the rest of her time with her father holding his hand as he slept. At 8:30 o'clock that evening, with his family at his side, Gilliam Wyatt Coffey passed away in his sleep at the age of 59 years and six months old. The funeral was held the following Saturday afternoon at the Baptist Church in Okanogan and he was buried in the Okanogan cemetery.

A sad year for the family ended on a high note with Minnie and Charlie adding to their growing family. Doris Jane Harrell was born December 8, 1913. Her birth was bitter sweet for Minnie. She was sad her Papa was not there to enjoy her growing family. She already missed him so very much.

Sarah Jane lived with Candus and Lee and was thankful Lee was always so willing to take the family into his home when they needed help the most.

Despite the sadness the family experienced while living in Spring Coulee, there was great joy too. The grandbabies continued to be born. In 1914, Cordie and Walter had another daughter, Alma Cook. This brought great joy to Sarah Jane. She appreciated God's gifts, and wished Gilliam had lived to see all the grandchildren come into the world.

The county had elections in 1914 to decide which town would be the county seat. The current county seat, Conconully was too far away from the railways, and not a practical choice. The decision was up to the voters, Okanogan or Omak as their new county seat. The over whelming preference was Okanogan. In April of 1915, they broke ground on the brand new courthouse and construction began. Charlie worked hard helping to build the new landmark. He was proud to be a part of the crew that would construct such a vital landmark to serve the people and local government. The beautiful Southwest style courthouse was completed in October of 1915. Times were good, and the future of the area was bright. There were more and more automobiles on the roads, a sure sign that people were more financially able to buy expensive luxury items.

The Lord continued to bless the family when Julie and Walter welcomed a son named Bynum Robbins. Minnie also had a baby of her own. Like Matt, Minnie also chose to honor the memory of her niece. They named their third daughter, Hazel Dovy Dean Harrell, arriving on December 4, 1915 just in time for the Christmas season. Minnie loved being a mama to her three girls and she loved being Charlie's wife. She felt very blessed that Christmas.

Although there was not as much work for Charlie in the winter months, he still managed to find odd jobs to keep his family fed. By spring, work was more abundant, and he was working longer hours. Every day, except on Sundays, Minnie set the table and waited for Charlie to come home from a long day of work. Her days were devoted to her children, and her evenings belonged to Charlie. They put the girls to bed after dinner and enjoyed their quiet time together. Often times, they would sit together in front of the fire place with a cup of coffee and visit. Just being together was enough for them. They would dream of the future ahead of them and make big plans. Charlie wanted to build on to their home and make it larger for their growing family, he wanted to plant trees on their place, have a vegetable garden, and eventually have more children, perhaps a son.

More children did arrive in the family in 1916. Larkin and Emma were blessed with a son they named Albert. Cordie and Walter had a son they named Clarence. Hoyt and Matt were also blessed to have another son, Frank born in Virginia. Sarah Jane was sad knowing she might never meet the children Matt had after leaving Spring Coulee. None the less, she felt very blessed and happy for Matt.

Minnie became very concerned about Charlie. He seemed to be tired a lot, and did not seem like the happy easy going fellow she married. He saw a doctor, but nothing was found to be seriously wrong. The doctor suggested he had a bug and to take it easy for awhile. Charlie seemed to be turning down a lot of job offers, and this worried Minnie. It was not so much that they desperately needed the money, but turning down any job was so unlike Charlie. However, Charlie reassured her that he was fine and not to worry. Minnie did worry, though. She wanted her sweet happy Charlie back.

Candus and Lee noticed Charlie's lack of enthusiasm, even going so far as to criticize his lack of interest in employment opportunities. Minnie was hurt by this and very disappointed in Candus and Lee that they would publicize their opinions on the matter. Charlie continued to work, even though most times he did not feel up to it. He knew he had a family to support, he tried to ignore the criticism and do the best he could to support his family.

In June, 1917 Larkin and Emma had a baby boy they named Henry. The family continued to grow that year with Julie and Walter having another little girl they named Bertha. It was another very productive year for the Coffeys and Cooks.

With World War I in full swing, Joe decided he would join the army. He was a PFC in the 361st Infantry, 91st Division. Five months after the United States declared war on Germany in 1917, the original 91st Infantry Division was activated at Camp Lewis, Washington. After ten months of training, the division was sent to France. Joe was wounded when shrapnel lodged in his hip during battle in the Argonne Forest. He would return home, but his company would go on to see action in Germany, Belgium and Italy.

By September, Charlie had become seriously ill. This time, the doctor's diagnosis was not encouraging. Charlie had a tumor on his prostate. They would attempt to remove it, but the prognosis was not good. Minnie held her daughters close as the doctor gave her the news she hoped not to hear. Charlie was dying. She was about to lose her husband, and her girls were about to lose their father. On September 24, 1917 Charles Martin Harrell lost his battle with cancer and died at the age of thirty five years, seven months and twelve days. Minnie was brokenhearted. Her beloved husband and best friend was gone. Her memory reflected back to Bertha Cone during that awful time when she lost her husband, Moses. Only now could

Minnie truly understand just how sad and empty a woman could feel after losing her husband.

Minnie and the girls were forced to move back to Spring Coulee. Lee gave her and the girls a cabin to live in on the backside of his orchard and Minnie washed clothes to earn a little money to provide for the girls. She felt guilty having to ask for help, but Candus and Lee were very open and accommodating as usual in their time of need. Candus loved Minnie's little girls, but was always especially close to Leda. The girls were always welcome in the main house with Candus, she loved being with them.

In the months that followed, Minnie felt a yearning to return to North Carolina. Without the happiness of having Charles in her life, her thoughts kept going back to the good times she had while living at home. She missed Callie very much and seemed to need her even more during her time of sorrow. She kept wondering if she would be happier living there, not that she would actually pack up her daughters and move away from her family, but she did have reoccurring thoughts of going home. Perhaps it was just the sadness she was feeling, she was not sure. But for some strange reason, she was not feeling at home in Okanogan any longer.

Candus and Lee's kindness and generosity really became evident by the following summer. Cordie's husband, Walter decided he did not want to be married any longer and abandoned his family. Cordie and their children, Grady, Oscar, Gladys, Alma and Clarence were suddenly alone to fend for themselves. Cordie always figured he would have a change of heart, come to his senses and return to them, but it never happened. Walter was gone, never to return home again.

Cordie was so thankful to Lee and Candus for allowing them to stay on their farm.

That year, Cordie's sixteen year old son, Grady decided to travel by train to California to find work. Cordie was not too keen about the idea but reluctantly allowed him to go. Several weeks later, they received a letter from Grady saying he was on his way home. Cordie was thrilled her boy was coming home, but tragically, Grady never arrived. As though he dropped off the face of the planet, he was never seen or heard from again. Tormented by his disappearance, Cordie hired a private investigator to find Grady, or to find out what might have happened to him. The investigator was able to track him to a logging camp in northern California, but was unable to locate any signs of him from there. Cordie was crushed. She could not help but blame the tragedy on Walter. Had he not abandoned them, she was certain Grady would not have left Spring Coulee looking for work. Her anger was over shadowed by grief and despair, however. She knew it was wasted energy to blame anyone, and tried to stay positive and hoped one day Grady would come home. Unfortunately, that never happened.

Again, tragedy would hit the family in less than a year's time. In March of 1918, Larkin and Emma's baby son, Henry died in his sleep. He was one year, three months and fourteen days old. They were devastated. There was no sadness like the ache of losing a child. Larkin and Emma grieved hard, and took a long time to adjust to the loss of their baby boy. Sarah Jane had suffered the loss of three grandchildren in less than seven years time.

Living at Spring Coulee brought the family a lot of joy, but it also brought its share of sorrow. The emotional ups and downs of life certainly took its toll on everyone. Despite the sadness, the family was blessed and very optimistic about their future.

Once a month, a traveling salesman from the Watkins Company would come to the farm selling everything from body soap and spices to cleaning supplies. Minnie liked Silas Townsend. He was always friendly and had interesting stories to tell. He loved to talk about his wife and children and all of the people he had met while out making his sales door to door through-out the county. It seemed he knew just about everyone. It was a good way to learn some gossip too, if you were into that sort of thing. Mr. Townsend was a good decent man, and although Minnie could not afford to buy anything extravagant, she always tried to save up enough money to purchase something from Mr. Townsend when he visited. Even the most insignificant purchase would do, she figured every little bit helped. After all, he too had a family to feed.

One day during his visit, he mentioned to Minnie of a farmer down near Pateros who was a widower with three sons. He asked Minnie's permission to tell this farmer, a Mr. Brownlee about her. Perhaps Mr. Brownlee would want to contact her? Minnie really was not ready for a relationship of any kind, she was still grieving so for Charlie. She knew a big part of her would always grieve for Charlie. But after a few months went by, Minnie suggested to Mr. Townsend that it might be a good idea for Mr. Brownlee to write her. After all, Minnie had three little girls to raise and having a father figure there for her girls and some financial stability might not be such a bad thing, if the man was a decent sort of fellow. She knew she had to move on with her life and did not want to depend on Candus and Lee forever. Although she could not imagine herself ever loving anyone other than Charlie Harrell, getting married and having her own place again was the only solution that made much sense at the time. Minnie consented for Mr. Townsend to give Mr. Brownlee her address so that he might write to her. Within ten days time, Minnie received her first letter from Mr. Brownlee.

It was a very warm and sunny Okanogan Valley morning when Mr. Townsend returned to the farm in Spring Coulee. It was July of 1918 and Minnie was scrubbing clothes on the washboard outside of the main house and hanging them on the line to dry when she saw Mr. Townsend's car coming down the road. The soft powdery dust was rolling up from behind his car all the way down their road. When the car stopped, the dust blew on past him and filled the air. Minnie was a little annoyed since she just hung her wash on the line, but Mr. Townsend was oblivious to the laundry or the dust his car had just kicked up.

" So, did you hear from Mr. Brownlee? I gave him your address."

She was now amused with Mr. Townsend. He was so eager to play matchmaker.

Minnie smiled and nodded her head yes.

"I'm so happy for the both of you," Mr. Townsend said.

"Well, thank you. We'll see how it goes from here. He seems like a nice man," she replied.

" He's pretty much in the same boat as yourself. He is alone with three sons. His oldest is near seventeen years old now and has pretty much raised the other two youngins since he was seven years old. It's a sad situation, alright. It's just not easy for a man to get along without a wife," Mr. Townsend explained.

"Yes, he explained all that, it hasn't been easy for him," Minnie replied with a smile. "It hasn't been easy for me either. I look forward to meeting Mr. Brownlee," Minnie paused like she lost track of her thoughts. "So what new items do you have for sale to show me today, Mr. Townsend?"

Mr. Townsend took Minnie around to the back of his automobile where all the merchandise was stored. Candus, Cordie and Sarah Jane came outside to join them. Minnie never had any intentions to say a word to them about Mr. Brownlee or the letter. She felt she would be judged for agreeing to write to Mr. Brownlee so soon after Charlie's death.

Later on, after she put the girls down for their nap, Minnie found quiet alone time to sit and again read the letter from Mr. Brownlee. She was impressed and intrigued, so she returned the favor with a long letter of her own. She posted it the next day and waited for a reply. She had learned from his letter that he was sixteen years her elder and had three sons named David, Robert and Walter. He played the fiddle for social events through-out the county and loved music. He owned a substantial amount of land for ranching in an area called Watson Draw on the hill above Pateros, Washington.

Minnie made sure she was the one who walked to the mailbox for the mail from then on. She did not want her sisters to see correspondence addressed to her from some strange fellow. How would she explain that? Within a week, Minnie had a reply from George Brownlee. Again, she reciprocated with a letter of her own. They exchanged letters this way for over a month. Minnie felt she was ready to meet Mr. Brownlee, but would leave it up to him to make such a suggestion first.

By now, Joe Coffey was settled back home and recovering from his war wound. The family was very relieved and grateful he returned home without a more serious injury. He found himself a nice girl named Neata to court, and they were getting pretty serious. Sarah Jane figured it was only a matter of time before another one of her children was married.

Sarah Jane and her daughters had no idea about Minnie's little secret, not until the day Sarah Jane decided to take a little walk for some fresh air and exercise and proceeded down to the end of the road to get the mail from the mailbox. While feeding the chickens, Minnie saw her mama in full stride headed for the mailbox. Minnie dropped the feeding bucket, grabbed hold of her skirt and took off running to catch up with her. Soon they were side by side at a fast pace.

"Child what are you doing chasing me down like this?" Sarah Jane asked.

"Oh, nothing Mama. Just thought I'd join you," Minnie replied while trying to catch her breath. "I'll run the rest of the way and get the mail for you."

Sarah Jane stopped walking and turned to Minnie. "The point of me walking was to actually go as far as the mailbox, Minnie. I could use the exercise. Candus and Cordie have been baking too many desserts lately, I'm starting to feel a little thick wasted, if you know what I mean."

"Oh, yes ma'm, I do… I mean I don't think you're fat Mama, I mean I think I could be gaining a few pounds myself," Minnie answered and then quickly sprinted ahead of Sarah Jane to get to the mailbox first. She quickly thumbed through the stack of mail scanning the return addresses. Sure enough, George W. Brownlee had sent her a letter. She distracted Sarah Jane so she could hide the letter. "Oh look, mama, there's a deer over in that meadow!"

Sarah Jane looked across the way in the meadow and Minnie quickly shoved the letter into her apron pocket. "I don't see a deer, it must have ran off."

"Oh, maybe so, mama. I thought I saw one," Minnie said as she walked back to Sarah Jane and handed her the stack of letters.

"What about the other one?" Sarah Jane asked.

"Other one, Mama?" asked Minnie.

"I might be getting old, child, but I am not blind. The letter you stuck in your apron, what's that all about?" Sarah Jane replied.

A warm feeling rushed Minnie's red face. She was not one to lie to her mama, and she was not about to start now. She had been caught red handed, it was time to confess.

"Well, ah…. Mama, it's from a friend. Mr. Townsend introduced us, kind of," she said tentatively

"Really? You don't say! So is she like a pen pal then?" Sarah Jane asked.

"Well, no, not exactly. Ya see, *she* is a *he*. And he is looking for a wife," Minnie replied.

"What the devil? What do you mean? Like one of them mail order brides?" Sarah Jane inquired with a very concerned look on her face.

"No Mama, it's not that impersonal. We've been exchanging letters for over a month now. Mr. Brownlee is lonely, he's a widower with three sons. He's a lot like me, Mama, but he's older with older children. We both lost our spouses and we have children to raise. He likes music too. He plays the fiddle, how about that! He has a farm too, and lot's of land."

"Older? What's older, Minnie Lee?" Sarah Jane crushed the mail in her hand and put her fists on her hips. She gave Minnie the look of a mother hen disciplining her chicks.

"Only sixteen years older, Mama," she answered in a soft voice.

"Hmmf, Sarah Jane snorted. I just can't let you run off with some old farmer with a bunch of boys you'd get stuck raising. You have to be careful about these things, Minnie."

"Mama, he's not some old farmer. He's only sixteen years older, and he's a very kind and sweet man. His older boy is practically raised. I wouldn't run off with anyone I didn't know or trust. I promise." Minnie reassured her.

"Let's take this slow, Minnie. I just don't want you making a mistake. You can't know this man by just writing letters. Where does this feller live anyway?" Sarah Jane asked.

"Pateros, or near Pateros. Up on the hill above Pateros, " Minnie answered.

"Minnie, we've been through some sad times since we've been in this part of the country. I couldn't bare anything happening to you or my granddaughters. You make sure you know what you're doing. Don't leap into anything because you feel desperate, you have a home here. You are far from desperate," Sarah Jane reminded her.

"I know, and I love you all for your love and support. I know it will all work out," Minnie assured her.

"It broke my heart when Charlie died, I hated seeing you so crushed and sad. I don't ever want to see you sad again, Minnie. I know you are a grown woman and can make your own choices. I love you very much, you'll always be my baby. I couldn't stand another heart break for you, or for this family," Sarah Jane said.

Minnie put her arms around her Mama. "I know, but I have to move on with my life, maybe take a risk or two. I know I have my girls to consider, but I promise we will be fine."

"I know you'll be, darlin'… I know it," her mama answered.

9 Meeting George Brownlee

Eventually, Minnie confided in her sisters about the letters to George Brownlee. Although they supported her, they were a bit apprehensive about him. George had business to attend to in Okanogan, so one sunny day in early November Minnie agreed to host George and his sons at her home in Spring Coulee.

Minnie was very nervous about meeting George, although she felt like she knew him very well already. They had exchanged a lot about each other in their frequent correspondence, but until she actually met the man would she know just how compatible they might be.

George arrived right about the time on which they had agreed. Minnie was impressed with his promptness and approached his wagon to introduce herself. He seemed a little nervous but quickly stepped down off his wagon, took off his hat and shook her hand. His three sons, Dave, Walt and Bob stepped down from the wagon and stood beside their father with hats in hand. Minnie noticed right away how tall and thin seventeen year old Dave was. He towered over his father but it was obvious he was George's boy. Dave desperately wanted Minnie to like them. It was time his father had a proper wife, and he needed a mother figure in his life despite the fact he was nearly grown.

Minnie liked George from the moment he stepped down off the wagon. He was quiet and reserved but very much a gentleman. She felt very comfortable talking to him about his farm, his life and his family. He was a handsome man, about five feet eight inches tall with a slight build wearing bibbed overalls and a straw hat. Minnie did not feel as if he was sixteen years older and they seemed to have a lot in common despite the age difference.

George Brownlee's parents were born near Strathaven, Scotland. He was the youngest of six children born to Andrew and Grace Brownlee. They were direct descendants of Thomas Brownlee, second laird of Torfoot, who fought with the Scottish Covenanters in the battles of Bothwell Bridge and Drumclog in 1679. Andrew, Grace and their daughter, Mary immigrated to America on October 20, 1858, arriving at Ellis Island aboard the S.S. Edinburgh. The family first settled in Illinois, but when George was 13, his family moved to Wessington, South Dakota to farm. There he later met and married fourteen year old Pearl Best.

To escape the harsh winters, George and his pregnant wife left South Dakota in 1901 to take farm land in Washington State. Shortly after their arrival in Waterville, Washington, Pearl gave birth to David Steven Brownlee on November 30, 1901. George and Pearl settled near Pateros, Washington in an area called Watson Draw to farm and soon more children arrived. In eight years time, Pearl had given birth to five children, Walter George on August 14, 1903 and Robert Andrew on October 27, 1905. Unfortunately, Pearl died when she was only twenty two years old on her husband's birthday, January 17, 1909 of consumption shortly after giving birth to twins. Sadly, the twins also died.

George's brother, Andy and his wife Bessie and their children as well as his father, Andrew had joined them in Washington State in 1904, homesteading on land near George's farm. George's mother,

Grace had died while they were still in Illinois. Without a close mother figure to help with the boys, George felt desperate enough to leave his farm and take the boys to Everett, Washington where they lived for two years with Pearl's parents, Nancy and Steven Best. Nancy and Steve had moved to Everett from South Dakota a few years prior. George had a wagon and horse team, so he went to work at the local docks in Everett hauling freight. The boys loved their grandparents, but hated being away from the ranch. One bright spot about living in Everett, however, was a chance to see a wild west show featuring Buffalo Bill Cody and Annie Oakley. They also were able to see horse racing champion Dan Patch. George appreciated the Best's help and hospitality, but eventually they returned to the farm. It was then up to Dave to help with the farm and take care of his younger siblings.

With his father busy on the farm, Dave pretty much raised Bob and Walt. His young shoulders carried a heavy burden caring for his brothers, sacrificing his childhood to help his father raise them. Dave cooked their meals, cleaned up the messes and had his own chores to do on the ranch. When something needed repairing, Dave did it. He was a good carpenter and loved to build and work with his hands. Often times, he would have to miss school to care for his brothers. Dave loved school, so having to miss even one day was very disappointing to him. To make up for his interrupted education, he read every book available to him. He had a great fondness for Abraham Lincoln and loved reading books about his life. He also loved to draw and was a very devoted artist, preferring to draw pictures of horses. Dave loved playing the guitar and was excited to know that he shared that common interest with Minnie.

George got along wonderfully with Minnie's daughters, Leda, Doris and Hazel. Since he had sons, he thought it was nice to be around little girls for a change. Minnie had baked an apple pie for the occasion, and they all sat at the table and had a piece with milk and coffee. Afterwards, the boys went outside and watched out for the three girls, giving Minnie and George some time alone to visit.

"You have nice boys," Minnie said.

"I have good boys, yes. They're a little rambunctious at times, but good boys," explained George. "It hasn't been easy without a mama for them. I know it's not fair to Dave that he had to take up the slack when his mama died. I can't help but feel guilty that his childhood was stolen from him at such an early age, but what could I do? I needed help and I can depend on that boy. He was so close to his mama. It nearly broke the boy's heart when she passed."

"I'm sorry that you all have been through so much. I feel bad that they've been without a mama for so long. My girls have been without their father for nearly two years now, but they are still young. I am fortunate though, I have a large family nearby and they help me look out for the girls," Minnie replied. "I'd like to see your ranch one day."

"Oh yes, I'd like that. We'll have to arrange that soon," George replied with eagerness in his voice. "I'd like that very much and I am happy that you want to keep in contact with me."

"Well that's just plain silly, Mr. Brownlee. You're a nice fellow, why wouldn't I want to see you again?" Minnie asked.

"It's been awhile since I've talked to a lady such as yourself. I've never had much time for courting and I know I'm a little rusty when it comes to this sort of thing. When that salesman suggested I write to you, to be honest I wasn't so sure I wanted to. But ya know, I am really glad I did," George replied.

George stayed for awhile longer, but being he had such a long trip back to Pateros, he could not stay for as long as he wanted to. He enjoyed meeting Minnie and they made plans to continue to correspond by mail. George wanted to arrange for Minnie to see his ranch soon, but with the worst of the winter looming, it could be months before that was possible. In the meantime, Minnie was eager to continue their mail correspondence.

Minnie and George kept the post master busy all winter. Putting a face to the letters now made it easier to feel closer to one another. Fortunately the winter was mild and by February, George felt he could easily make the trip to Okanogan and Spring Coulee. On February 16, 1919 George and his boys arrived at Minnie's cabin. They were there to get her and the girls and take them home. Their first stop was the main house to tell the family goodbye, and from there they went straight to the courthouse in Okanogan where a civil wedding united them as husband and wife. George took his new family home to the farm near Pateros, he was a married man again.

George's boys were thrilled to have a mother figure in the house, especially Dave. He felt the weight of the world had been lifted from his shoulders. He was sure God had sent an angel to save them all. Having little sisters would be something to adjust to, but the boys did not mind. They looked forward to being one big happy family, and that's exactly what they were.

Minnie was very fond of George, and she felt in time she would come to love him like she did Charlie. It was a marriage of convenience and necessity, but George was a good decent man and she trusted her feelings about their union. She knew it was the right thing to do for her and her girls. She had no regrets, and felt very fortunate that Mr. Townsend had made the suggestion they start writing to each other.

Not long after Minnie arrived on the farm, she met George's brother, Andy and his wife, Bessie, and their children, Bertha, Siegel, Maynard, Fleetice and Lowell. Never having the desire to be a farmer, Andy had sold their acreage on the hill to George and left to go to barber school in Spokane. He and Bessie later moved to Pateros and he opened his own barber shop in 1906. Andy and George's father, Andrew had a place just up the draw from George's place, but he died of influenza on February 10, 1914.

Minnie wasted no time putting a woman's touch to the farm house. In the spring, she opened the doors and started cleaning. She transplanted yellow rose bushes from Andrew's homestead, planted lilacs and seeded nasturtiums in the window boxes. She hung drapes, beat the dust out of the rugs and spruced the place up. Minnie loved the challenges of being a mother of six now, and she was quite happy being a farmer's wife. When she baked pies, she would open the kitchen window. The aroma filled the outdoors and soon her home was full of hungry pie eaters eager to dig in and enjoy a piece. She loved cooking and baking for her family. They certainly seemed to appreciate her, and being appreciated was all she ever wanted from them.

A lifelong Baptist, Minnie suddenly found herself attending a church of another faith. The Brownlees, being one of the original family members of the Church of Christ in Pateros, were well established in their own congregation and Minnie would never dream of asking anyone to change faiths on her behalf. She was now George's wife, and a member of the Church of Christ in Pateros. She felt very comfortable from the beginning when she attended church with her new brothers and sisters in Christ. The Pateros Church of Christ was founded by early settlers of the area, including the Nickell, Adams and Miller families.

Minnie was never one to waste anything. Besides collecting rain water, she used dish water to water all her flowers and the Virginia Creeper vine that grew at the end of the house. She enjoyed the fresh fruit from the apple, peach and Italian prune trees, berries from the Elderberry and goose berry bushes that grew nearby, the nearby rhubarb and the grapes that grew in the arbor. There was a fresh spring nearby that came down from Andrew's place they used to irrigate their very large vegetable garden. She had pie cherry and apple trees on Andrew's old place that she also picked. Despite the hard work of caring for a large family, Minnie felt very fortunate to be living there.

Minnie loved watching and listening to the many birds the ranch had to offer. Some of her favorites were the meadowlark, the dove, the grouse and the pheasant. In the summertime when the wind was still, you could hear every bird on the hill singing, along with the chickens, the rooster and the occasional bellow of a cow. Minnie felt at peace on the farm and although she worked hard raising a large family, she was very happy and content.

Down the road about two miles lived a couple named Jim and Polly Gobat. Polly's maiden name was Best, and she was related to Dave, Bob and Walt on their mother's side of the family. Minnie befriended Polly and they became very close. Other than her sisters, Polly was the closest friend she had since moving to Washington. They visited often and became great friends.

On July 26, 1919, Joe Coffey married Neata Townsend, daughter of William and Elizabeth Townsend. They purchased a home on Pogue Flats and Joe worked for Lee Cook. He also witched for water and did a little logging with Larkin. Joe also helped build the large "wooden ditch" that ran forty five miles from Oroville to Okanogan. The large wooden trough was used to provide irrigation water to the area.

It was forty three miles from Spring Coulee to George and Minnie's farm on the hill above Pateros. Sarah Jane was happy for Minnie, and impressed with the ranch. She knew Minnie had made the right choice and it was comforting knowing she and the granddaughters were so well cared for.

The year 1919 was a busy and blessed year for the family. Besides the two marriages, Julie and Walter had another baby girl they named Pauline. Good fortune continued the following year when Larkin and Emma welcomed son James Coffey to their family and Joe and Neat had their first baby, Letha May Coffey born May 19, 1920.

10 Raiding the Chicken House

Dave put his talents as a carpenter to good use by renovating the family home. He added a living room with an upstairs so the boys had their own bedrooms. He enlarged the porch, screened it in and installed a wood burning stove. He also added two more bedrooms downstairs and built a large front porch where he hung a large porch swing.

In the summer months when it was so hot, Minnie used the screened in porch for canning her vegetables and fruits. Using the wood burning stove on the porch was much more comfortable than building a fire indoors.

Dave was twenty-one years old before he ever took a ride in an automobile. He had a love for any type of machinery, and it would be only be a matter of time before he had an automobile of his own. In the 1920's he bought a 1915 Ford Model T and the old days of farming with horse, plow and wagon was replaced when he purchased an old McCormick tractor.

George played fiddle for social gatherings through-out the county, especially during the summer months. He was well known county wide for his talents with the fiddle. Minnie enjoyed tagging along to watch, but never had the desire to play in public. Dave was becoming an accomplished guitar player himself, and played with his dad. Sometimes Andy would join them on fiddle and family friend, Zeb Howell would occasionally play banjo with them. Dave's mother,

Pearl was also a fine fiddle player, so he received his musical talents from both sides of the family.

Minnie's brother, Larkin decided to move to Malott. His wife, Emma made extra money taking in laundry. Using a scrub board, she worked hard scrubbing clothes clean to earn money for the family's new home. Eventually, she earned enough money to pay for an acre of land in Malott. The family rented an area home until their new home could be built on the acre of land they had purchased. Since Malott was on the road to Okanogan, it was convenient having the family there when Minnie and George needed to do business in Okanogan. Leda and her sisters loved to stop in Malott and visit with Larkin and Emma's children. Leda and Edna were very close in age, and very close in life. They were cousins, but theirs was a close special friendship they would share through-out their lives.

Leda was now ten years old. Taking her height and her looks from her father, she was a small child with brown hair and beautiful dark brown eyes. Leda, Doris and Hazel loved to make mud pies and play in the water trough. When Leda felt she needed eggs for her baking, not wanting to get in trouble herself, she would send Doris to the chicken house to collect her required ingredients. George Brownlee was an understanding man, however, he could be very strict. To him, eggs were serious business. Eggs were sacred to a farmer, and you just did not mess with a farmer's eggs, not even for mud pies. Knowing this, Leda was not about to get caught, so she sent Doris to do her deed. Doris did not quite understand the severity of her crime, so she was always willing to do the shopping for their baking needs. She had managed to dodge Mr. Brownlee up until then, but one day her luck ran out. Mr. Brownlee walked into the chicken house as Doris was walking out with an arm full of eggs.

"Doris!" he yelled at her.

A startled Doris jumped, wet herself and dropped two of the eggs. They splattered on the floor at her feet. At this point, she realized she was in big trouble. Hearing him yell from outside the chicken house, Leda took off running for cover.

"Yes sir?" Doris quietly responded.

"What do you think you're doing? You don't take eggs from the chicken house. We can't have eggs for our breakfast if you play with the eggs. You're not to take the eggs from the chicken house, do you understand?" he barked at her.

"Yes sir, I won't do it again," she replied as she returned the unbroken eggs to the nests.

"Now get on out of here and don't be pulling such nonsense again, ya hear me?" he asked her.

"Yes, I mean no, I will never do it again," Doris replied as she ran out of the chicken house crying.

Later that evening, still upset over the egg caper, George complained to Minnie regarding what had transpired in the chicken house that day. Minnie pretended to be a little upset with Doris, but deep down, she had herself a giggle. Mr. Brownlee would get over it, he always did.

It seemed to Leda that she was always in trouble with Mr. Brownlee. However, that did not stop her from having her share of fun, often at Doris's expense. One day while playing in the field where the sheep had been pastured, Leda had a wonderful idea to play a trick on Doris.

"Close your eyes and open your mouth, I'll give you something to make you healthy, wealthy and wise," Leda said to Doris.

Much to Leda's surprise, Doris was very willing to play along. She stood in front of Leda with her mouth wide open and eyes shut. Leda stuffed sheep poop into her mouth, sending Doris gagging, spitting and crying all the way back home.

Leda knew she would be in trouble once Doris reached the front door, but the little practical joke was well worth whatever punishment she might get for it.

Minnie appreciated Dave's talents as a carpenter, and she loved having the larger more convenient home that accommodated the family as they grew older. By December of 1923, she was exceptionally grateful for the larger home when she found out she was having a baby and was due the following summer. This was quite the surprise, especially to the older children, but they were very excited about the news of a little brother or sister.

Minnie wrote to her mama and told her and the family of her good news. They were elated and very excited to know there would soon be another family member. They made plans for a visit in the spring. Minnie was very happy and had grown to love and cherish George.

Their life was a farm life, but in many ways, they were richer than most.

George and Minnie welcomed baby son, John Charles Brownlee into their family on July 16, 1924. Big brother Dave had the honor of naming the little one. He named him after John Charles Fremont, the military officer that he had enjoyed reading about. The family adored John. His sisters loved having a real life baby to play with and take care of. Everyone appreciated having a baby again in the family.

Matt and Hoyt also welcomed another son, Mastin Cook in 1924. Sadly, he was another grandchild born in Virginia that Sarah Jane would never know.

On January 12, 1925, Joe and Neata had their second child, a daughter named Ruth Elizabeth Jane Coffey. Sarah Jane was pleased for the name sake and to have most all of her grandbabies near.

On May 2, 1925, Walt married Betty Shaw. He was the first of the three brothers to be married. They bought land southwest of George's place and George gave Walt a few head of cattle to get his ranch started. On January 16, 1926 they had a daughter they named Elaine. Sadly enough, after living only three months the baby died. On November 3, 1926 they had a boy they named Floyd but there were complications. Betty had a difficult time with the birth and the baby suffocated during delivery. This was a very sad time for the family.

At three years old, John had dark brown curly hair and blue eyes. He was a handsome little man and his family adored him. Just when they were getting use to the idea of having a little tike to look after and love, Minnie had another astonishing announcement for her family, she was going to have another baby. Although surprised by the news, the family was very happy there would soon be another baby on the ranch to chase after.

Joe Coffey lost his wife of eight years when Neata passed away from tuberculosis on November 17, 1927. She was only forty two years old and left behind her young daughters, Ruth and Letha. Unable to care for the girls alone, Joe was forced to ask the family for help. The girls went to stay with their grandmother in Spring Coulee, but this arrangement was short lived when the family lost Sarah Jane on March 31, 1928. Sarah Jane died in her sleep from an apparent heart ailment at age seventy four years, two months and twenty six days old. She was laid to rest next to her beloved Gilliam in the Okanogan Cemetery. The backbone and strength of their family was gone. Cordie ended up caring for Joe's girls after Sarah Jane's death. Again, Candus and Lee's farm in Spring Coulee was a haven for those family members needing a soft place to land when they needed help the most.

Still saddened from Sarah Jane's passing, Minnie gave birth to Grace Opal Brownlee on May 14, 1928. She was a pretty little blonde hair blue eyed girl and the apple of George's eye. Minnie was well blessed but also felt very sad that her mama did not live long enough for Grace's birth.

The ranch was growing and doing well so Dave decided to take on a side business. He purchased a delivery truck and started the Brownlee Dairy, delivering milk to local families. George and his sons stayed busy, and sometimes they needed extra help with the farm.

Occasionally, George would hire Ace Best to help get in the hay. Ace was Polly Gobat's father, and a relative to Dave, Bob and Walt on their mother, Pearl's side of the family. He was a nice man, and could laugh at himself, so Bob and Walt poked fun at him a bit and played the occasional joke on poor old Ace.

One afternoon Minnie sent Bob out to the field to round up all the men helping with the hay, it was time to take a break from the work and eat a proper meal. George, Dave, Walt and Ace came in from the hay field, washed up in the wash tub Minnie always provided for them outside, and then went inside to have their meal. Ace had a habit of taking his wad of chewing tobacco out of his cheek and saving it for later while he ate his supper. On his way into the house, he would place his tobacco up in the open frame work of the porch just before he entered the house.

One day, Walt and Bob decided to play a little trick on poor old Ace. They waited until all the men were inside the house and Ace was eating his supper. They took Ace's tobacco down out of the rafters, pulled open the wad of chew and added chicken manure. They rolled the wad back up and placed it back up in the framework where Ace had left it earlier. Bob and Walt went inside to eat their meal, snickering about what they had just done.

After supper, the men filed out of the house and were standing around talking when Ace reached up and grabbed his tobacco. Walt and Bob looked at each other and grinned. They could hardly wait to get a reaction out of poor Ace.

Ace put the wad of tobacco in his mouth, shoved it over to his cheek with his tongue and continued talking with the men as usual.

Still anticipating a reaction, Walt and Bob looked at each other again and snickered. Much to their dismay, Ace kept visiting with the other men and never reacted to the chicken manure he was now obviously chewing on. Several minutes had passed and the men were preparing to go back to the hay field when suddenly Ace stopped talking. Obviously there was something on his mind.

"Ya know, I smell chicken shit," he proclaimed. Bob and Walt turned away so no one could see them holding back their laughter.

Ace continued talking, and chewing on his tobacco. A few minutes later, Ace once again stopped talking, wrinkled up his brow and looked around as though he was looking for something.

"Ya know, I really can smell chicken shit. I smell it so plain, I can almost taste it," he complained.

Bob and Walt, barely containing their laughter, had to quickly walk away before laughing in Ace's face. They briskly walked toward the hay field leaving the other men behind. No one but Bob and Walt knew what they had done, and as far as they knew, Ace continued to enjoy his tobacco and never did spit it out that day.

The dairy and the ranch were doing so well, most days there were filled with a lot of activity. People would help with the stock or help get the hay in, or occasionally folks would stop in for a quart of milk.

Often times five year old John would go out into the field with his dad and work with the other men. John rode in the wagon or sit on the back of a horse, he did not care as long as he was with his dad. One day there was a group of men at the barn unloading hay from one of the wagons when Mr. O'Toole stopped at the ranch to visit and joined them in conversation.

Mr. O'Toole had a reputation for saying what he thought, no matter how crude it was. Minnie did not care for the man, and did not want him around her children. In fact, she did not want him around her husband either, but she had no control over such things. Most men took what he had to say in stride and half the time ignored most of what he had to say.

On this particular day, everyone seemed to forget the presence of little John who was sitting quietly in the back of the hay wagon closely listening to every word the men were saying. George was trying to converse with the men and work at the same time, not thinking about what was being said in front of John. Mr. O'Toole started talking about a wedding he recently had attended and said a few crude things that were inappropriate, especially in front of a child.

Later on during their evening meal, the family was seated at the table eating, passing food around and having conversations about their day. Eager to get a conversation of his own started like a big boy, innocent little John decided he would contribute to the conversation by repeating something he had heard that day.

"Wasn't that funny about that woman getting the bone put to her last night?" John said with a laugh.

Minnie stopped chewing and dropped her fork. George choked on his chicken. Dave, Leda, Doris, Bob and Hazel stopped chewing their meal and sat quietly trying not to laugh. John, sensing he said something wrong, stopped laughing and looked around at everyone.

Minnie was obviously not amused in the least. She slammed down her dinner napkin and left the kitchen.

"Mr. Brownlee, come here please!" Minnie yelled for George from the living room.

"Gracious me, I've had it now," George said under his breath as he got up from his chair and walked to the living room.

Not able to control their laughter any longer, the older children burst out laughing.

11 Two Weddings In the Family

The start of a brand new decade was underway and a lot had changed since Minnie moved to the hill. The county was growing and the fruit and ranching industries were thriving. Walt and Betty learned they were about to have another child. After suffering the loss of two babies already, a lot of prayers were said for this pregnancy. On July 23, 1931 Glen Allen Brownlee was born. Walt and Betty had their healthy baby boy, and were very happy.

It was always exciting having a new baby in the family. Even with the older children, there was never a dull moment on the ranch. When Grace was five years old, she looked up to her older sisters. Leda, Doris and Hazel loved taking advantage of Grace's innocence. One day while the older sisters were getting ready for church, they were each taking turns using a hair wave cream. The hair wave product had a peculiar odor, this was evident when Grace walked into the room to watch her sisters groom themselves for the day. Grace approached the dresser where Leda had set the product and stuck her little nose down closer to get a better whiff.

"Pew, that stuff stinks," Grace proclaimed with her little nose wrinkled up. "What is it?"

"It's canned farts," Leda replied.

Doris and Hazel smiled at the joke and continued to get ready for the day. Because it was common place to tease Grace, no one thought another thing about what was said to her until the next day. A neighbor, Mrs. Campbell dropped by the ranch for a visit and was seated in the living room talking to Minnie when Grace walked out of the bedroom carrying the can of hair wave cream. Doris, Hazel and Leda were in the kitchen doing dishes but could hear everything said in the living room.

Grace proudly lifted the can of cream up to Mrs. Campbell. "Mrs. Campbell, would you like to smell some canned farts?" Grace asked in her sweet innocent voice.

Mrs. Campbell raised her eyebrows and her eyes grew wide. She looked at Minnie who sat speechless with her mouth open. An embarrassed Minnie gently led Grace with her canned farts out of the living room and back into the bedroom. By this time, Mrs. Campbell was laughing so hard, she was snorting. Leda, Doris and Hazel quickly and quietly slipped out the back door and made themselves scarce.

Grace believed anything her big sisters told her. For instance, they told her the cream they put on their legs to remove hair was called Chinese snot. As far as gullible little Grace was concerned, that's exactly what it was, because her sisters told her so.

Most Sundays after church, and after the supper dishes were washed and put away, the evenings were spent listening to the radio. Whether it was a favorite radio program, or the news, near the radio was a favorite place for the family to gather in the evenings. Occasionally George and Dave would play their guitars together. Bright and early Monday morning, it was back to work like normal with their usual routines around the ranch.

It was during these family gatherings that Minnie first started noticing a certain exchange of affection between Doris and Bob.

Minnie, not knowing what to think of this behavior, chose not to say much to anyone, thinking perhaps she was just over reacting. Bob and Doris did seem to enjoy one another's company more as they grew older, not that they were ever inappropriate. They did, however, seem unusually close, even smitten with one another in a romantic kind of way. Minnie hoped she was just imagining things.

Just when Minnie was trying to understand this romantic like behavior with Bob and Doris, did she notice the same behavior with Dave and Leda. She thought it very odd, but again, did not say anything for fear it could just be her imagination.

Early in the year of 1933, Minnie's suspicions were verified when Doris approached her and confessed her love and affection for Bob.

"Bob? You can't love Bob, not in the marrying kind of way. He's your brother, for goodness sakes!" Minnie replied.

"He's my step brother, not blood relation. We love each other!" Doris answered.

"But what will people think? You can't marry Bob. This isn't decent," said Minnie. "I love Bob, as a son. I can't approve of you marrying your brother..... I can't accept this!"

Despite her fondness for Bob, Minnie tried to sway Doris into breaking if off with him. She even tried reasoning with Bob. Finally, she told George about the family scandal and he made an attempt to discuss the situation with Bob. But to no avail, they were in love and intent on marrying. Their union made Minnie very unhappy and she was determined not to accept it in the least. Often times she would have bouts of despair just thinking about it and would cry and become depressed. George, although not happy about it either, did not take it to heart as Minnie did.

Minnie and George were still not happy when they finally reluctantly agreed to their children's union, but they would not stand in the way of their happiness or their marriage. On March 21st, 1933 Bob and Doris were married. They took nearby land on the hill and started their own farm. As with Walt, George helped them get started by giving them a few head of cattle. Eventually, Bob would also raise sheep.

Minnie was not privy to any of the likely rumors she was sure must be going around regarding Doris and Bob's marriage. She felt it best she did not hear any of the rude gossip that their marriage surely had caused. After all, although unchristian like, it was human nature to talk about such things even if it was none of their business. Minnie tried not to care, although it did bother her that she and George could be put in the position of defending the children for loving each other.

In their younger years, Leda, Doris, Bob, Walt and Dave had attended a one room school house on the hill known as the Watson School district, but none of them had made it past the eighth grade. Hazel, on the other hand rode the bus to town and attended school in Pateros. She would later graduate from Pateros High School in 1933. Out of the six children, she was the only one that finished high school and went on to further her education. After high school graduation, she left for business school in Spokane. Within a year's time, Hazel finished business school and accepted a position at the county prosecuting attorney's office in Okanogan. This is where she met her future husband, Emery Vandiver.

On May 7, 1934, Doris and Bob's first child was born, a son they named Andrew Morris Brownlee. Having a new baby in the family certainly made it easier for Minnie and George to accept Doris and Bob's union. In fact, the controversy had long been forgotten.

Just when they thought all was right again with the world, Dave had an announcement of his own, his intentions to marry Leda.

"What's wrong with you children? Are you all trying to give me heart failure?" Minnie asked Dave upon his announcement. "First Doris and Bob, and now you two. I know you aren't blood relation, but you live in this house as brother and sister."

George shook his head in disbelief. "Oh my Lord," was all George could say.

"I've loved Leda for a long time, Dad. I've never wanted to marry anyone but her. I've waited for her, and she's old enough to make up her own mind, and I want to marry her," Dave proclaimed. "I'll never love anyone else."

George and Minnie knew, like with Bob and Doris, there was no talking them out of marriage. Minnie especially had a difficult time accepting the news, but eventually made peace with their decision. On August 12, 1934, David and Leda were joined in marriage. They had their ceremony on the lawn at Uncle Andy's home in Pateros, Washington. Church of Christ preacher, David Nickell officiated.

Leda's cousin, Edna would be married to Frank Nickell just three days later. They attended Leda and Dave's wedding and had photos taken with the newlyweds on the big lawn at Uncle Andy's house.

Leda and Edna were cousins, best friends and would forever celebrate wedding anniversaries in August.

Dave and Leda spruced up George's original house up on the hill above the ranch and made it their own. It was nice having their own home, yet still being part of the ranch. Dave loved the ranch and was happy to be there to help his dad with the ins and outs of a working busy ranch.

In the spring of 1935, Leda contracted smallpox and was very ill. Unfortunately, she was pregnant at the time and gave birth prematurely to a deceased infant boy. She had been five months along in her pregnancy and he was a fully developed infant. They placed the little angel in a casket made from a shoebox and buried him up the draw on Grandpa Andrew's land. It was a very difficult time for Leda, not only being sick, but also losing her baby. She was thankful for the love of her family, especially her mom who was there with her through a most difficult time in her life. Minnie was very diligent taking care of her daughter and burying her grandson was heart breaking.

With the support of her family, Leda made it through that awful time, both physically and emotionally. In June, Leda discovered she was two months pregnant when Edna was seven months pregnant with her first baby. The cousins had a lot to be thankful for and were happy to be sharing this blessed time in their lives together.

Leda and Edna were not the only family members with blessed news to share. On July 9, 1935, Walt and Betty had another healthy son, Wayne Richard Brownlee. On August 1, 1935 Edna and Frank had a baby girl they named Katherine Rae Nickell.

Also in August of 1935, Julie and Walter's daughter, Bertha, or Bert as she was affectionately known, was selected as rodeo queen by the community who cast their votes in stores in down town Omak prior to rodeo weekend. Bert was one of seven young women entered in the contest, and was crowned the very first queen of the Omak Stampede Rodeo in Omak.

The family continued to grow, and the next generation of Brownlees and Coffeys were being born, however, the year also brought some bad news for Julia and the family. On November 10, 1935, Walter Robbins passed away at age sixty three years of age.

Leda's turn to contribute to the growing family came on January 25, 1936 when she and Dave welcomed a girl of their own, Ellen Marie Brownlee into the world. Ellen was born in Brewster at a maternity house with Dr. Randolph bringing the baby into the world at 2:00 PM.

Leda and Dave could not wait to take their baby home, but there was a problem. Back at the ranch waiting for them was eight year old Aunt Grace with a bad case of chicken pox. Dave had to leave Leda and baby Ellen in town at Uncle Andy and Aunt Bessie's home until it was safe to bring the baby home to the ranch. Once Grace was well, Leda brought her baby home for the first time.

Four months later, on May 18, 1936 Doris and Bob had their second son, Philip Douglas Brownlee. On August 22, 1937 they had their first daughter, Lorraine. Bob did not want to give Lorraine a middle name, he wanted her to use her maiden name as her middle name once she married one day.

Needing more room for their growing family, Dave decided to move out of the homestead house and into a larger house that was conveniently located on the ranch and closer for his daily chores. He remodeled the milk house and with his talents as a carpenter, turned a modest out building into a comfortable home for his family.

On March 6, 1938, Edna and Frank Nickell had a boy they named William. On October 3, 1938, Dave and Leda had a baby boy they named David Eugene Brownlee. Again, Edna and Leda had new babies in common and enjoyed good times together as new mothers.

Hazel and Emery Vandiver were married in 1939, with three year old Ellen serving as their flower girl. Hazel and Emery had their first baby, a girl named Janice Ailene Vandiver on October 3, 1941. Both sides of Minnie's family continued to grow and be blessed.

Living on a ranch out in the country, a child had to have a pretty good imagination. Often times, they had very few toys to play with. At best, they could hope for a toy truck, a doll, or a cap gun at Christmas. A country kid learned to make the best of any situation and to use their imagination and be grateful for everything they had.

Grace's imagination brought a little bit of Broadway to Brownlee Hill. She loved to put on plays for the family and friends in the area. She would gather her cast and practice nursery rhyme plays of her own adaptation. One of her favorites was Little Miss Muffet, staring Ellen Brownlee as Little Miss Muffet and cousin Earl Best as the spider. They would practice until Grace thought her cast had their lines and marks down perfectly, and then put on a show for family and friends. Although Ellen was not fond of being a Broadway star herself, she reluctantly participated in Grace's productions. Grace used a bed sheet for her curtain and stretched it from the house to the ivy vine. Her stars earnestly waited for the curtain to open and the play to begin. Her audiences usually included her mom and dad, Leda, Dave and their David, brother John, Polly Gobat, and sometimes Doris and Bob or Walt and Betty and their children. It just depended on who was at the ranch and available during show time.

12 A Country At War

In 1941 the world was at war, and on December 7th the Japanese forced America's hand. John was a junior in high school and safe at home for now, but Minnie feared he would be drafted once he was eighteen and out of school. The thought of him going off to war terrified her. The world was a frightening place, and every able man was called to serve.

It was a confusing time too if you were a child. Not understanding what war was, or why everyone was so upset, Leda and Dave's innocent three year old toe headed son, David was having a difficult time understanding it all. He wondered why the Japanese would want to harm this lady named Pearl Harbor.

Candus suffered a stroke that year and it left her physically and mentally impaired. Lee, not wanting to deal with her illness on his own, asked that the family take care of his wife during this ordeal. Cordie had enough heartbreak to deal with most of her entire adult life, the latest tragedy she had to contend with was helping to raise her grandchildren. Her son, Oscar's wife died leaving him with four boys and two girls to raise. Cordie moved to their farm and helped Oscar raise the children.

Minnie and Leda realized it was up to them to care for Candus during this difficult time after her stroke. Most times they cared for her at home in Spring Coulee, but they also brought Candus back to their ranch where Minnie and Leda divided their time spent taking care of her. She was completely dependent on others, unable to move on one side, she had to wear diapers that needed changing often. She needed help in feeding herself, and her sweet kind personality turned mean, angry and incorrigible. Taking care of her was anything but easy, especially for Leda with two small children to care for, but Candus had always been there for her family so now it was time for Minnie and Leda to help her when she needed them the most. A young Grace resented the time her mother spent with Candus, and it did not help matters that due to her illness, Candus was so ornery to everyone. It was indeed a difficult time for all the families involved.

Candus and Leda had always been close. Leda was sorry her daughter, Ellen would never know the Candus she remembered as a child. She would never know how kind, generous and patient she was. Instead, she knew her daughter would remember the angry and bitter Candus she would come to know as a five year old child. Because they once were so close, Leda felt compelled to care for her now. Dave was very understanding and supportive through the process. He was more than willing to take on extra work at home so Leda could be with Candus as often as possible. Likewise, George was very understanding when it was Minnie's turn to look after her sister.

Sadly, Ellen's memory of Candus would be jaded with the unpleasant side of her illness. Ellen was not exposed to the worst of what it was like to care for her, but she did see a very angry and demanding woman taking up her mother's time. Just as the family sat down to dinner, Candus would inevitably need something. This would be the time she usually insisted that someone give her an enema. It was not so much that she needed the enema that bothered everyone, but it was all in the timing, and the fact she was so demanding with no regard for those who tried to care for her. Unfortunately, Leda knew these were the memories Ellen, Grace and John would recollect about their Aunt Candus, when they truly did not reflect the true spirit and character of the woman Leda grew up loving and admiring.

Caring for an ill Candus was a sad time for Minnie, but her large family provided love and support for her and kept her sadness away as she stayed busy caring for and loving them all. Despite how difficult it was, Minnie tried to keep a sense of normalcy for her youngest children by encouraging them to do well in school and to have time for their friends. Grace spent a lot of time with her cousin, Ruth. Ruth often stayed at the ranch with Grace, or Grace stayed with Ruth in Okanogan. They were inseparable, especially in the summer months.

Feeling the need for more living space, Dave once again started remodeling one of the ranch's many out buildings. This time, he chose the old chicken coop to renovate. It did not take him long to turn the one room hen house into a fair sized home for his family. After living in a smaller home for much of her young life, Ellen thought the new house felt like a mansion and was eager to move in.

Dave had a great sense of humor and loved to laugh. He tried to find humor in most everything, although you would not always know just how much something amused him until later on when he was replaying it in his mind. He could laugh about something for days, out of the blue you could see him laughing and not know what was so darn funny and he would have to explain. A funny card, a joke someone had told, or something stupid someone did, if it was humorous, Dave relived it for a while and laughed about it for days. He had peculiar but loving nicknames for his children too. If he gave you a nickname, that meant Dave loved you, you could be sure of that. His nicknames usually came from books he read or radio stories he had listened to. His daughter Ellen, he gave the nickname of Alveric McEatwey, but eventually just called her Alveric. As for son David, he called him Buddy Hist, but usually just called him Buddy. Later on, when David was older, he was given a new name, Stew Fullgerston Jones, or Stew for short. Dave thought his son fit the description of a character he read about in a book, right down to his white hair color, so he thought it an appropriate nickname for his toe headed son. John also had a nickname for his nephew, he called him Swede.

Minnie enjoyed her growing family. She kept in contact with her family in Spring Coulee and visited them when she could. The family also visited her on the ranch as often as possible. At any given time, there were children running amuck on their place, brothers, sisters and cousins were plentiful, ranging from the very young to adolescence. Walt and Bob's children were among the frequent visitors there to play dolls or cowboys and Indians and hide and go seek with their cousins and friends.

Living in the countryside out in remote areas could be hazardous in the dry summer months when the green spring grasses turned parch and brown. It was especially so by the end of the summer, sometimes going three to four months without a drop of rain. The arid grasses burned like dry paper when caught on fire and there was not much to stop a raging grass fire from spreading to thousands of acres before it could be stopped. One such fire occurred late that summer. It raged on like the monster it was, coming from clear up the Methow Valley near an area called Gold Creek. It came up over the hill and was headed towards the backside of Brownlee Hill and loomed above the town of Pateros. The school was back in session after summer break, so the children were evacuated and sent home. The ominous orange glow of the mighty fire was just over the hill and it filled the skyline with dark choking smoke. Teenager John Brownlee worked with the fire crew to fight the mighty blaze that scorched many acres.

Everyone on the hill figured the Brownlee ranch was the best place strategically to take a stand against the fire that first night. Dave, Leda, George and Minnie welcomed all who came to stay at their place, trying to accommodate everyone during this frightening time. They monitored the fire well into the night taking shifts sleeping on the floor of the ranch house when exhaustion over came them.

Fortunately for them all and the fire fighters working hard to put the huge fire out, the winds shifted and they were able to get a hold on the raging inferno. Minnie figured God saved their ranches that day. If the wind had continued to blow as it did, many farms would have been swallowed up in the raging fire. There was plenty of destruction in the fire's path, but fortunately the fire never made it to the hill, or to town.

George Brownlee suffered a stroke late in the summer of 1941. This was shocking news, as George was always such a healthy man. The family rushed him to the hospital where he spent nearly a week being treated and evaluated. Luckily, the stroke was not as bad as it could have been. He did suffer some mild paralysis, however, and had difficulties with his speech from that day on.

Dave knew the ranch was too much for his dad after his stroke, so he purchased a home in town for his father, Minnie, John and Grace.

The house was just at the bottom of the hill and at the edge of town, a very convenient location for visiting them during their family trips to Pateros. Knowing his dad's life would never be the same again, Dave took over the ranching duties and moved his family into the larger ranch house. He expanded the 3,000 acre ranch when he eventually leased five acres from the U.S. government and then purchased more land from Jim Gobat, Floyd and Chet Tupper. He also paid the back taxes on the Bill Gray place and took possession of that land as well. Later on, known simply as the Gray Place, it was once owned by a Pinkerton detective named William Gray. He was in the area looking for a couple of men wanted by the agency and had purchased the land to retire there. Knowing they were hard working family men trying to make an honest living and raise their families, he did not have the heart to pursue the wanted men any longer and never took them in. Gray later sold the acreage to a man from Pateros who could not pay his taxes, and the county took possession of the land. Dave would eventually grow winter wheat, spring wheat and oats.

John graduated from Pateros High School in June of 1942. He knew being drafted was an imminent reality. Minnie did not even want to think about the fact he could be called to serve. Jack Nickell, a classmate of John's from Pateros High, was sent to the European theater. John wondered if he would land in Europe or the Pacific, only time would tell.

The summer after graduation, John took a job in Portland, Oregon with Kaiser in the shipyards. He learned to weld and helped build troop transport boats to be used in the war. The first and only transport boat he saw launched was during a dedication ceremony by Eleanor Roosevelt. The transport boat slid down into the Columbia

River where it broke in half and subsequently sank. It was during his employment with Kaiser that he received his draft notice. He was ordered to report to a dismemberment center in Seattle on Christmas Eve, 1942 however, his basic training would not begin until the following April.

On July 15, 1942, Minnie's sister, Candus passed away in her home. At sixty six years, eight months and twenty two days old, the eldest child of Sarah Jane and Gilliam Coffey was gone. It was a difficult time for her siblings, but considering the suffering she had endured, it was a blessing God took her home. They laid her to rest in the Okanogan Cemetery.

As the war progressed, the government brought German and Italian prisoners of war to the United States to work in labor camps. One location chosen was the small town of Malott where they brought in Germans to work in the apple industry and various construction jobs in the area, such as construction of the Omak airport. Before the war would end, more than 450,000 Germans and Italians would be in the U.S. working in the POW camps. Every state in the union had these camps, with the exception of North Dakota, Nevada and Vermont.

Cordie's daughter, Alma married Joseph Wagner and they soon welcomed a daughter, Josephine Gayle Wagner born on September 23, 1942. A new baby in the family was a good diversion in a time of anxious uncertainty. The baby was named after her father, but they called her Gayle.

John was assigned to the 155th Engineer Combat Battalion out of Camp Cooke, California and was to report on April 12, 1943. It was very difficult to say goodbye when he left for boot camp. Minnie was a strong woman, but seeing her only son go off to war was more than she could bear. A part of her soul went with him that day. For days she was morose, depressed and unable to function normally. Although George was sad and worried too, he tried to stay strong for Minnie. Grace, now a freshman at Pateros High missed her brother very much. She had a steady beau since 8th grade named Art Nordang and she tried to stay active in school and busy with friends to keep her mind off the war news. It was indeed difficult for the entire family. Not since Joe Coffey's enlistment had a family member served in a world war. They knew they might not see John again for years, if at all. Saying goodbye to her son was the single most difficult thing Minnie had ever done. When anyone mentioned John's name in conversations, Minnie could not help but cry.

From basic training, John was sent to San Luis Obispo from December 1, 1943 to April 30, 1944 for amphibious combat training. John was then sent to Camp Beale, California until June of 1944 where he received further combat training.

In the evenings after supper, Minnie would sit in her chair in front of the radio and listen to the news of the war and cry for John. Her granddaughter, Ellen would often sit in silence with her as she wept. Because she was so young, she did not understand the full impact of the situation or why her grandma was so distraught. To comfort her, the only thing she knew to do was just be with her. Ellen loved her grandma very much and hated to see her so sad and upset.

Before John left for his service in the Pacific, he made a coded name chart for the family. The Army would not allow him to tell the family where specifically he would be sent, nor would he know until the last possible moment where he might go. However, once he got his orders he planned to write home and give them a code where he would be going. For instance, they would know from the chart if John asked about Grace, he was going to Tarawa. If he asked about Andy, he would be going to Guam, if he asked about David he was going to Borneo, if he asked about Ellen he was headed for the Philippines.

On February 23, 1943 Emery and Hazel had their second baby, a boy they named James Ronald Vandiver. Unfortunately, Jimmy was born with a heart ailment and within a year of his birth, he would require an operation if he had any chance to survive. Surgeries such as what he needed were only experimental at that time, so the odds were against him surviving at all. Because Hazel and Emery could not afford a cross country trip, or the surgery itself, The Shriner's paid for Hazel to take Jimmy to Johns Hopkins Hospital in Baltimore, Maryland for the surgery he desperately needed. Although the heart was repaired, the operation was not deemed a success. The child had a stroke during the long procedure and suffered irreparable brain damage. Tragically, Jimmy was severely physically and mentally impaired. Not long after his surgery, Hazel and Emery moved from Okanogan to Coulee Dam, Washington where Emery took a security job at Grand Coulee Dam.

John's battalion shipped out to the Hawaiian Islands on June 24, 1944. They were there until August 11, 1944. Ironically, John would spend most of his time in the Pacific aboard a Kaiser troop transport boat, built in Portland, Oregon. Needless to say, it made John very apprehensive being in this boat, and ultimately he would spend over 300 days at sea before the war ended.

John and his company were first sent to Guadalcanal, however, as they were about to approach the island by amphibious landing, their orders were rescinded and they were diverted to another location. Another engineer company was sent to take their place. This replacement company barely made it to shore before they were all killed. If John's company had proceeded with their original orders, they would have been wiped out. It would appear fate stepped in and saved John and his company that day.

The government had a rationing program in place during this great time of need when the war effort took precedence. Everything citizens of the U.S. once took for granted, they were now finding more difficult to purchase. Each person was given ration coupons or tax tokens, and was allowed to purchase controlled amounts of items on certain days using their coupons. Tires were the first thing to be rationed in 1942 and eventually anything made from rubber was interrupted. To conserve for the war effort, gasoline was rationed with gasoline cards and citizens could only buy gasoline a few times a week if they could prove they had a need for it. The national speed limit was reduced to save on gasoline and rubber tires. Other items such as meats, butter, shortening, jellies, jams, silk, coal, bananas, dried fruits, canned milk and penicillin were also rationed. Some items such as sugar were distributed to families depending on the number of people in a household. Although Minnie lived in town now, she still had access to the fruit trees and berry bushes on the ranch, so not having the sugar she wanted for pies and canning was quite frustrating for her. It was frustrating for the rest of the family too, because they missed her pies. Times were tough and every family felt the impact of the war in some way.

News of the war really hit home when everyone learned about the capture of Jack Nickell. Information was sketchy, but the word was he was in a German POW camp. Knowing most did not survive the camps, this was not good news at all and further fueled the fear for John's well being. Jack Nickell was a brother to Edna's husband, Frank. Also, Jack and Frank's father, David was the preacher who officiated at Dave and Leda's wedding. Frank and Jack had a brother, Lee who was also a friend to the family.

There was yet another family tie to the war, a cousin Minnie never knew. His name was Dwight David Eisenhower, or Ike, and he was a five star general and Supreme Commander of Allied Forces in Europe during the war. Ike's father was from Pennsylvania and his mother from Virginia, so Minnie never knew him, although they were born the same year. There were various ways to spell the name including Isenhour, Icenhour, Isenhower, etc. Ike's family preferred the spelling Eisenhower, however, the original spelling was Eisenhauser. Minnie and the general were cousins through their grandfathers.

Minnie's mind was preoccupied with John being a world away. She worried about him constantly and it was difficult to go months without hearing from him. Living in town was very different for Minnie. She had less work to do, and more conveniences, but she still missed the ranch. George was getting along well. He had a small amount of paralysis on one side and in his hands, and was very frustrated that he was no longer able to play the fiddle. He cherished playing the fiddle, but was forced into the realization he would probably have to give it up for good. Fortunately, his speech was only slightly affected. Minnie felt bad that he could no longer play the fiddle, but she felt very blessed he was regaining his strength and doing so well. She thanked God for sparing his life and giving him the courage to get well. Recovering from a stroke, even a minor stroke, was a challenge for anyone. George had good days and bad days, but for the most part he was doing well and Minnie was thankful she still had her husband. Walt and Bob were good to stop by and check on their father. George enjoyed having company, especially family.

Since Walt was the school bus driver, he was in town quite often. If Minnie needed anything, he was always available to help out. He was a good, honest and considerate man who loved to laugh and play a joke or two.

Even when Walt was not driving the bus, he spent a fair amount of time in town visiting with friends at Uncle Andy's barber shop or having a meal at his favorite restaurant. There was almost always a reason to be in town. He always enjoyed being around people and felt the need for social interaction.

When Dave and Leda brought Ellen and David to town for groceries or supplies, Ellen always knew how to find Uncle Walt. She would seek out his truck which was usually parked in front of the restaurant. While the rest of the family was busy with their shopping, Ellen would walk over to the restaurant to find her uncle. After all, he was always good for an ice cream cone and a laugh.

Ice cream was always a good tool for bribing a child. One day while riding on the school bus with Uncle Walt, Ellen accidently hit her head when the bus was forced to come to an abrupt stop. Walt could see the tears starting to form in Ellen's big brown eyes. He hated to see her cry, so he used her love of ice cream as a deterrent.

"Ellen, if you don't cry, I'll buy you an ice cream when we get to town," Walt promised Ellen.

Fighting back the tears, "Ok," was her only reply.

Several minutes later, believing that her Uncle Walt had forgotten his promise about the ice cream reward, she decided to speak up with a gentle subtle reminder.

"Chocolate would be nice," she said.

Walt had a good chuckle to himself and proceeded to town for ice cream.

Walt's wife, Betty, on the other hand rarely left home. She knew every cow on the place by name, she knew which cows were bred and which were not. She knew every calf on the ranch and which cow the calf belonged to. She knew how many heifers, bulls and steers she had on any given day and she could give you an accurate count of all her cattle and the chickens in the coop. She knew the history of every chicken, chick and rooster on the place. She kept the ranch's books and did the taxes. Walt completely relied on her memory, knowledge and book work to keep the ranch running smoothly. There was no doubt, Betty was the ranch manager. Not only was she a good mother to Glen and Wayne, she was also a great cook.

Dave and Leda purchased the house next door to Minnie and George the summer of 1944 and moved their family to town. They thought it would be nice living in town next to their folks with the modern conveniences, but still had their ranch on Brownlee Hill with all their cattle to care for. Dave under estimated how difficult it would be to live in town and have to feed and care for his livestock every day. Even though they no longer had their dairy, the ranch was still a lot of work. Ellen and David enjoyed walking to school instead of riding the bus, and being in town was so much more convenient for them. For Minnie and George, it was very helpful having them live so near, but they realized how difficult it was on Dave and Leda to care for the ranch when they lived in town.

John's company was sent to Ulithi Atoll on September 23, 1944 to build an airstrip. They remained there until October 26, 1944. Up next was the island of Peleliu. They approached the island of Peleliu on November 1, 1944 by amphibious landing. The American fleet had pretty much wiped out the Japanese Navy in the Philippine Sea, so there was no longer any need for an airstrip on Peleliu. However, no one called off the invasion and Peleliu was one of the more costly landings of the war. The island would have the highest casualty rate of any island in the Pacific War before it was said and done.

John enjoyed R and R in New Caledonia from January until April of 1945. It gave John time to relax and write home. Minnie and George were thrilled to receive a letter from him as it had been a while since he had the time to write to them. They were happy but fearfully curious where his orders would send him next. John asked about Ellen in that letter, and this meant he was going to the Philippine Islands. Ellen did not understand the code, or even care where the Philippine Islands were. She was just thrilled that Uncle John had asked about her and felt very special that he would think of her.

John's company was sent to the eastern Philippine island of Leyte on June 17, 1945 and stayed there until September 17, 1945. The war now over, John was sent to Aomori, Honshu, and Sapporo, Japan before returning home. He was part of the occupying forces sent to Japan to help rebuild their infrastructure. The Japanese people were very afraid of American soldiers, and of John. He finally befriended a Japanese family there by offering them his rations and they reciprocated by inviting him to dinner.

In the summer of 1945, John Brownlee came home from his service in the Pacific. The generation that saved the world was welcomed with open arms. The world celebrated the end of a long, costly and horrific era. Minnie was so thankful to have her son home again. For days, she waited on him hand and foot. She figured after everything he had been through, he needed a lot of rest and pampering. She thanked God over and over again for the gift of her son's return. Much to everyone's surprise, John's classmate, Jack Nickell also returned home. It was a miracle he survived the horrors of a German prisoner of war camp, and Jack gave God the glory and credit for his survival.

One afternoon when the family was gathered, John brought out his army foot locker. It was full of souvenirs and clothing from Japan. Ellen and David sat on the floor and curiously watched as uncle John spread out all the items from the large locker onto the floor for everyone to see. They were most intrigued by the Japanese swords and the silk clothing. Everyone enjoyed holding the souvenirs from John's ordeal in the Pacific.

John made a habit of frequenting the local bowling alley in Pateros. There was a certain young lady who worked there that he fancied. Her name was Beverly Bonar, and her folks owned the place. Bev was a senior at Pateros High, and she had always liked John. She was happy he to see him again after his years away serving his country.

It was not long after she graduated that Bev and John were married and they moved into a small apartment in Pateros. John, along with his brother, Bob bought a wheat ranch together near Chelan called Washington Creek Ranch. The business venture was not as profitable as they had hoped, so John took a job with the state highway department.

Hazel and Emery moved from Coulee Dam to Eugene, Oregon and on July 23, 1946, they had their third baby, Nancy Lee Vandiver. Minnie was a little disappointed that Hazel and her kids lived so far away. She missed seeing her grandbabies growing up. However, on April 15, 1947 Doris and Bob had a daughter they named Jean. Once again there was a baby in the family to pamper and enjoy. Like with her sister, Lorraine, Jean was not given a middle name. She would use the name Brownlee as her middle name once she married.

Dave and Leda sold their house in Pateros and moved back to their ranch on Brownlee Hill. It was just too difficult for Dave to live in town and have his cattle on the hill. Minnie hated to see them move back to the ranch, but was not surprised. She understood how difficult it was to maintain two places and be so far from the ranch at feeding time. She knew she would see them whenever they came to town. Ellen and David started riding the school bus again, but they did not mind. Uncle Walt was the school bus driver and they always enjoyed seeing him every morning and after school.

With everyone's minds barely off the war, the family was a little blindsided that autumn with the tragic news of a death in the family that was not so expected. On October 16, 1946, Julie's daughter Pauline Payne was found deceased in the bathroom of her home. Her husband, Guy found her unconscious and was unable to resuscitate her. Pauline suffered from a heart ailment, so her death was not a huge surprise, none the less, the loss of a child hit Julie and Walter hard and it was very difficult to accept her passing. Pauline was not quite twenty eight years old.

The government rationing program did not completely end until 1954, but more and more previously rationed items were becoming more available to Americas and everyone was appreciating items once forbidden or rationed during the war. Food items especially were welcomed back into the homes of Americans again, one being sugar. America loved its sugar, and it was probably the single most missed food item during the war. There was nothing like a cold iced tea with a little sugar if you preferred, or a tall glass of lemonade with sugar to tame the tartness of the lemons. Sugar was plentiful now and Americans took advantage of it. Items such as Kool-Aid drink mix were popular again. During the war, fruit acid and dextrose rationing actually slowed the production of Kool-Aid. After the war, the demand for Kool-Aid was so high, the company who manufactured the powdered fruit substance could hardly keep up with the demand.

One fan of the Kool-Aid drink mix was young David Brownlee. Leda allowed David and Ellen to have the drink, but because she was not so keen on the taste of the concoction herself, Leda would always add fresh lemon to the water and powder mix to give it more flavor. Having lemons was another luxury they did without during the war, so making a pitcher of Kool-Aid with lemon was a treat for them.

One afternoon David asked his mom if he could make some Kool-Aid.

"Sure, go make a pitcher, but don't forget to put in some lemon," Leda responded.

"Shall I put in half the lemon or the whole thing?" he asked.

"Oh, just use the whole thing," his mom replied.

The family was sitting outside visiting and enjoying the weather when David proudly bounced out of the house with his pitcher of Kool-Aid. He joined the rest of the family, setting the pitcher down on the small table near his mother's chair. A surprised Leda saw an entire whole lemon bobbing up and down in the Kool-Aid pitcher. She tried her best not to laugh, but once Minnie and the rest of the family saw the bobbing lemon, it was most difficult not to laugh out loud. Of course, David was not amused that everyone thought what he did was so funny so he hurried away crying. He would later return to have a nice cold glass of Kool-Aid with his family, it was just too tempting to stay away for long.

Grace and Arthur Nordang's courtship had endured since the 8th grade. Now graduated from high school, they started seriously planning a life together. Grace was Princess Pateros in the Wenatchee Apple Blossom Festival that spring. She and Art attended classes at Central Washington University at Ellensburgh in the autumn. However, after a year, Art talked Grace into leaving school and returning home to Pateros. Grace worked in the apple industry and Art worked on his dad's apple farm in the Methow Valley near Carlton, Washington. Grace married Art on December 12, 1948 at the

Church of Christ in Pateros. All of Minnie and George's children were now married.

Now a married man, Art took over his dad's apple farm, and he and Grace moved into his parent's home in the Methow Valley. His parents, Arthur senior and Ada moved down to Pateros. Art would later start his own long haul trucking business as well. Life was good, and about to get better. On November 13, 1949 they had their first baby, a son they named Gregory Arthur Nordang. Soon after, on September 2, 1950 John and Bev had their first child, a daughter they named Lerin.

Emery and Hazel moved their family to Tacoma, Washington where he took a position managing a cemetery. However, they had not lived there long when Emery asked Hazel for a divorce. A sad rejected Hazel returned to the hill for support and to be with those who loved her most. She stayed with Dave and Leda for a short while, but eventually returned to her position at the Okanogan County Prosecutor's office. She and her children lived in Lee Cook's house in Okanogan and her daughter Janice attended school in Okanogan. Lee, now remarried, had sold his Spring Coulee orchard and moved to town. However, he was often gone and needed someone to look after his place, so this was a good solution for both he and Hazel. By then, Cordie too had made the move to town. Lee saw to it she had a home of her own and no Coffeys or Cooks were left living in Spring Coulee.

A year later, Hazel decided to take her children and move back to Eugene, Oregon. Knowing that times could be difficult for an unmarried woman with children, Dave tried to talk her out of the move, and promised to help her if she would only stay near so family could help her and the children. Hazel was determined to go, and she felt Oregon was where she needed to be.   Once again, Leda and Doris said goodbye to their sister and Minnie said goodbye to her daughter as she moved away from the family.

Callie wrote to Minnie at the end of December to tell her of Uncle Tilden's passing. He died on December 26, 1950 at age seventy four. Minnie was sad to hear the news and wished she could be with Callie to comfort her. She had hoped to see Tilden again one day, but it was not meant to be.

13 A Tiny Surprise

Minnie and George hosted a family reunion at their home the summer of 1952. It was wonderful to have her family together, but the most important guests of all were from Virginia. Matt and her daughter, Hazel made the trip west to visit Minnie and attend her family gathering. Minnie and George's small lawn and house were over flowing with Coffeys, Cooks and Brownlees. For Minnie, it was a dream come true to have all of her family together at her home. This would be the first time she saw her sister since Matt left Spring Coulee forty one years ago. Minnie was very pleased that Matt was able to make the long journey west. Matt and Hazel met and visited with a lot of cousins and they had a wonderful visit with Cordie, Julie, Lark, Joe, Minnie and George. Not knowing when or if she would see Matt or Hazel ever again, Minnie felt their two week stay was much too short and hated to see them go home.

For Minnie, this would be a cherished event in her life that she would always look back on with fond memories. The summer of '52 was a special one, alright. It had to be one of the best summers of her life. A lot had changed since Minnie arrived in Washington State. Her children were all now grown with families of their own, and the grandbabies continued to be born. John and Bev had their second baby late that autumn, a boy named William George Brownlee born on November 17, 1952.

Unfortunately as time went on, Minnie experienced the unavoidable reality of losing her sisters. The Lord giveth and the Lord taketh away. And at the age of seventy three, He called Cordie home on April 11, 1953. Etta Cordelia Cook was laid to rest at the Okanogan Cemetery near her daughter, Hazel who was so tragically killed in the wagon accident years before. If you asked her, Cordie would say she had a blessed life, but out of all of Sarah Jane and Gilliam's children, one would have to say Cordie had the most difficult and saddest life of them all. She experienced a lot of joy, but she had more than her fair share of tragedy too. In her lifetime, she raised children from three families and suffered the tragic loss of two of her own and a daughter in law. Her husband left her alone to raise their children, and if not for Lee Cook and the support of her own family, life's burdens would have been much more difficult for her to bear. Minnie always thought it unfair for Cordie to endure all the hardships she did when she was such a good, caring and kind woman. Minnie would greatly miss her sister and was grateful that Matt had the chance to visit with her sister the prior summer.

Eight days later, God gave back to the family with the birth of another baby. On April 19, 1953, Art and Grace had their second baby, a daughter they named Suzan Marie Nordang.

There was another princess in Pateros that spring. Ellen was selected Princess Pateros for the annual Wenatchee Apple Blossom Festival celebration. Minnie's daughter, Grace was the first family member to have the honor, and now her granddaughter had the honor of representing the town of Pateros in the festivities.

Late that summer Dave and Leda decided it was time to move back to town. Uncle Andy and Aunt Bessie had moved to Seattle the previous year and were renting out their large Pateros home. Dave offered to purchase the historic home from his uncle and he gladly accepted. Having family there was much more appealing than renting the beautiful two story home to strangers. The house was originally owned by K. K. Parker, and was one of the first built in Pateros. For years it was the only property in town with shade trees.

Dave loved being a rancher, but as he grew older, he felt it might be time to try living in town again while they had the opportunity to buy Andy's home. He did not sell off his cattle right away, instead he made the daily excursion to the ranch to feed and care for his herd. Eventually, however, he did sell the cows but kept the land. Ellen started her senior year that fall. Living in town and walking distance from the school made it easier for her and David to attend school and after school activities.

Sadly, another of Sarah Jane and Gilliam's children was soon gone. The family said goodbye to Sibbie Julia Robbins on October 27, 1953 at the age of seventy six years old. It was very difficult for Minnie losing both sisters that year. She was a bit sad and lonely longing for how things once were, but the love of her own children and grandchildren helped her through the bad times. Despite losing her sisters, she felt well blessed. Her only remaining sister now was Matt, and she was thankful for her brothers, Larkin and Joe. She vowed not to take them for granted and made sure the families were together for special occasions and holidays.

Life certainly had its ups and downs and although it certainly was never easy losing a family member, there was always great anticipation and celebration when a new baby was welcomed into the fold. Larkin and Emma's daughter, Edna and husband Frank were a little surprised to find out they would be having another baby, and on August 18, 1954 Edna gave birth to son Larry.

Indeed life is certainly full of surprises and in late summer of 1955, Dave and Leda found out they were having a little surprise of their own. Only in their wildest dreams did they think they would ever have another baby, but sure enough, Leda was two months along. Although they fully comprehended the miraculous blessing of the news, they were also very apprehensive about having a baby at this stage of their lives. Their eldest child would be twenty years older than the last. At fifty three years old, Dave was not thinking of having more children of his own, his thoughts were more geared toward having grandchildren soon and was very disappointed in the pregnancy.

Naturally, Minnie, George and the rest of the family were very shocked to hear the news but were very thrilled and anxious to soon receive the newest member of the family. Grace and Art had some contributing to do of their own. Soon after Dave and Leda's announcement, they too proclaimed they would be having a baby of their own due in May. Minnie was so happy knowing she would have two new grandbabies in the spring.

Leda and Dave's baby was due in April of 1956, however, they were devastated when their baby boy arrived two months premature. Perry Steven Brownlee was born February 24, 1956 weighing four pounds and four ounces. He soon lost down to a critical three pounds, which was distressful news for his anxious parents. Because he was so tiny he spent most of his first days in an incubator fighting for his life with very little human contact from his parents. Leda could reach inside the incubator through the openings at the side and touch her tiny son. She could adjust his covers, but was not able to hold him. His tiny frail body endured painful daily injections of vitamin K in the back to nourish him, and the family was constantly warned of the potential complications, such as blindness, caused from the incubator. The needle they used to give him the daily injections was enormous, as long as the length of his little body. At one point, they were fairly certain Perry would not even survive. Dave and Leda thought the nursing staff had given up on Perry and were waiting for him to die. There were times Leda would find him uncovered and cold. She was constantly covering his little body in an attempt to keep him warm and comfortable. Leda, not able to hold her tiny son, kept vigilance by his side and eventually worked a shift at the hospital's nursery to care for all the babies just so she could be with Perry and care for him. She ached to hold him and eventually as he grew stronger, she was able to remove him from the glass enclosure he knew as home for the first weeks of his life. She spent many hours holding him and rocking him to sleep. Leda always felt that interaction with him is what gave him strength and the will to survive. Five weeks later, he turned the corner and his prognosis for survival was good.

Although not allowed in the nursery, Minnie visited her grandson in the hospital when she could. She was heartbroken that he had such a struggle to survive in the beginning of his life, and she also appreciated all that Leda and Dave were going through during this very difficult time. It was a time of prayers, and a lot of worry for them all.

In the beginning, Dave considered Perry an unwanted accidental pregnancy, but witnessing what his tiny baby went through in his fight to survive, his perspective of him changed in a powerful way. Perry was his little fighter and he quickly bonded with the tiny infant. He adored his son and was awe struck by his determination to live. His sheer will to survive was inspiring, and he was Dave's little miracle. He cringed and even became angry every time they stuck one of those long invasive needles into Perry's back. It broke his heart seeing the pain his tiny son endured.

Once Perry weighed five pounds at five weeks old, he was allowed to go home. Dave and Leda were thrilled to finally take their tiny baby home. With all the hours spent at the hospital worrying over him now behind them, they were anxious to take Perry home and share him with the rest of the family.

On May 23, 1956 Grace and Art welcomed their third child, Martin Lee Nordang into the world. They called him Marty, and he was a healthy baby. Minnie thanked God he was full term and healthy. After seeing the struggle little Perry went through at the beginning of his life, it was a relief that Marty's birth was not complicated. The boys were close in age and would grow up together as friends.

Bob and Doris had moved their family off the hill and were living just north of the town of Pateros. Bob had a barn and hay field behind his house and Dave often times helped him get in his hay or helped with other chores he might need help with on his place.

One hot August day, Dave stopped in to see his brother. Bob needed help getting the hay in, so Dave offered to join a small group of men gathered at the house to give him a hand. Dave was a strong man and it was nothing for him to lift the heavy bales of hay and toss them on the wagon pulled behind the tractor with little effort. The tractor was left parked facing down hill as Dave was throwing the last of the bales on the wagon. Suddenly, the tractor began to roll.

Bob saw his brother lunge for the tractor and yelled at Dave, "Just let it go!"

Instinctively Dave quickly jumped on the tractor in an attempt to stop it, but his foot slipped as he stepped up on the run away tractor and Dave fell under the tractor's largest wheel. The mighty wheel of the tractor ran over his shoulder and chest. The trailer tongue had an unusual U shaped dip to it, and as Dave's body cleared the large tire, he was then caught up under this odd shaped tongue and dragged down the hill, his foot badly mangled in the process.

Miraculously, the heavy trailer loaded with several tons of hay jack-knifed and came to a sliding stop inches before reaching his battered body. Had the trailer run over him, it would have surely killed him. Dave lay in agony on the ground between the tractor and the trailer. Bob ran to his brother and screamed back at the men for someone to get help.

Bob's son, Andy was walking out to the hay field from the family home and heard their screams for help. He quickly ran back into the house and called Doctor Harold Stout, and then he called his aunt Leda to tell her of his uncle's accident.

Immediately after receiving Andy's phone call, Ellen scooped up her tiny brother in a blanket and she and Leda got into the car. They raced to the field where the accident occurred, arriving about the same time as Doctor Stout. Still holding her little brother in her arms,

Ellen ran to her father's side and bent down to check on him. He had blood coming from his nose and mouth, and was in obvious pain.

Trying to catch his breath, Dave attempted to reassure his daughter. "Don't you worry, I'll be ok. I'll be fine now, don't you worry."

Trying to hold back the tears, Leda knelt down by her husband as the doctor checked him over. Seeing the immediate need to take him to the hospital, the doctor had the men help Dave to his car and he drove him to the hospital. A very concerned and scared Leda followed close behind the doctor in her own vehicle with Ellen and baby Perry.

Dave had broken his shoulder and bones in his chest, and had also suffered breaks in nearly every bone in his left foot. After several days in the hospital, he was allowed to come home. Dave was in pain for a long time after that awful day in August, but very thankful to be alive. He was in a walking cast and his arm was in a sling for many weeks, but despite his handicap, he cared for his baby son while Leda worked at the nursing home. He knew how awful it could have been and counted his blessings. He thanked the Lord and Doctor Harold B. Stout for taking care of him that day.

Just six months prior to the accident, Doctor Stout had delivered Perry and helped save his life. He was a dedicated doctor, and well respected in the community. He was the last of the country doctors who actually made house calls as a traveling physician. He helped found the Brewster hospital and the Brewster Community clinic. If a patient needed him, he made every effort to get to them, whether it was driving his Plymouth, a tractor, a horse drawn sleigh or a ferry, he made every attempt to be there for his patients. The family was very grateful and fortunate to have him as their physician.

14 Returning Home

Minnie longed to return to North Carolina to visit the family she left behind. Sadly, Uncle Tilden was gone, but she desperately wanted to see Aunt Callie and her sister, Matt again. She always felt that a part of her past was tugging at her to return home. So, Minnie began planning a trip back east in September of 1956. A very eager granddaughter, Ellen would take a break from her cosmetology job and go as her traveling companion.

Lee Cook gave Minnie and Ellen traveling money to help with their expenses. Minnie would ride the train back across the United States, but would not be returning to North Carolina right away. The plan was to stay with Matt and her daughter Hazel in Ashland, Virginia and from there drive to North Carolina. They also planned to see Washington D.C., Virginia Beach and various other sites of interest. Matt's daughters, Hazel and May planned to be their chauffeurs and would take them any place they desired. This was a once in a lifetime vacation, and they planned to see as much of the area as possible.

Minnie was very excited about seeing her sister, something she was not so sure would ever happen again once Matt left Pateros the summer of 1952. It had been four years since Matt attended the family reunion. Minnie also looked forward to seeing Hazel again and meeting Matt's other grown children. She felt sad that she had missed out on most of Matt's adult life, and Matt had missed out on being with their family, especially in the last years of their mother's life.

Minnie excitedly told everyone about her travel plans. Her friend, Polly was very happy for Minnie. She knew how Minnie longed to return to North Carolina, but more importantly, she was very happy that Minnie would have the opportunity to see her sister, Matt again.

As their plans started to unfold and arrangements were made, Minnie became very anxious for their cross country adventure to begin. George would be looked after by the family, but Minnie did feel a little guilty leaving him behind. He knew this was a tremendous opportunity for Minnie, and she might never have another chance to return and visit the home from which she came so many years ago. George did not believe he could travel well, and he was very happy Ellen was traveling with Minnie.

Minnie enjoyed Ellen's company and felt she would be the perfect traveling companion. They were always close and both appreciated each other's sense of humor. Minnie loved to laugh, so she and Ellen were very compatible. One particular late summer Sunday, not long before their trip east, Ellen and Minnie sat side by side on the same church pew. Other family members, such as Leda, Dave, David and others joined them on the same long wooden bench. Church was serious business, alright, but when Minnie found something to be humorous, she laughed. Nothing, not even Sunday worship services could keep her from a good chuckle if she found something to be amusing.

About five rows ahead of them, Mr. Wooten sat that day. He was a peculiar little man, but very proper with a serious nature about him. Poor Mr. Wooten started coughing during the sermon. Realizing his annoying cough was disturbing his fellow parishioners who were attempting to hear God's word, he decided it was time to take his noisy cough outside. He stood up and started walking toward the back of the church to make his exit. Just as he got about even with the pew where Minnie and Ellen were seated, Mr. Wooten coughed into his hanky and very loudly passed gas.

"What was that?" Minnie quickly whispered.

Attempting to keep a straight face, Minnie glanced over in Ellen's direction. When Ellen saw Minnie look her way, she lost her composure and began to giggle. The timing of the noisy deed and her grandmother's reaction to it were priceless. They both tried to muffle their laughter, after all, they were in church. The harder they tried to be quiet, the funnier it became. Just as they would calm down, one would start laughing and get the other giggling again. Needless to say, the rest of the family sitting on the pew were not sure what was so funny and kept giving Ellen and Minnie "the look", the glance a mother gives a naughty child in church when they are not behaving. Seeing Minnie so amused was funny in itself, and Ellen thought she might have to excuse herself. Finally, they both regained their composure and got themselves under control, or so they thought. It was then that Mr. Wooten returned, walking past them to take his seat. Minnie and Ellen tried desperately to quiet the laughter, but the sight of the man was all it took to set them off again.

Ellen loved being with her grandmother and was anxious for their adventure east to begin. Other than leaving home to go to beauty college in Seattle, she had never really been that far from home before. The chance to travel to the east coast was a wonderful opportunity for her, and she was thrilled to share the special time with her grandmother. All of her grandmother's stories of her life as a girl growing up in North Carolina were about to come to life, and she was very anxious to see where she grew up. It was definitely a trip of a lifetime for both of them. Although she would miss her little brother and the rest of the family, Ellen knew she would love the journey east with her grandmother and it would be an event in her life she would always cherish and remember fondly.

Little Perry was growing strong and Dave was healing from his tractor accident. Indeed, 1956 was a year to remember. Perry's birth was a blessing, but nearly losing him, and watching him fight for his life, took its toll on everyone. They were all very grateful Perry survived and enjoyed watching him get bigger and stronger every day. He was gaining weight and seemed very happy and content with so much life in his big beautiful blue eyes.

Ellen adored her little brother, and with Perry healthy and her dad on the mend, she felt comfortable leaving for North Carolina with her grandmother. After all the planning during the summer, the day had finally arrived for her and Minnie to catch the train.

As Minnie told George goodbye, she knew he would be in good hands with Grace caring for him. Art drove Minnie and Ellen south to the train station in Wenatchee that morning. They could not wait to board the train that would take them on their much anticipated journey. The autumn colors were bursting with orange, yellow and purple colors on a lovely September day. Minnie and Ellen enjoyed following the beautiful fall colors from one side of the country to the other. The weather was cooler, but still very pleasant and mild.

While on the train, Minnie spent a lot of time reflecting and thought a lot about those days spent traveling west with Charlie and her family forty five years prior. Although the journey west was at times difficult, she had very fond memories of her travels as well. She thought about how much her life had changed since that time so very long ago and she wondered if she would find her old home much the same as it was when they left it behind.

After having a four hour lay-over in Chicago, their three day journey finally ended in Richmond, Virginia. Matt's daughter, Hazel and her husband Johnny Bass met them at the train station and drove them back to their home near Ashland, which happened to be conveniently located next door to Matt and Hoyt's home.

After four years, Minnie was reunited with her sister again. Hazel lived on one side of Matt and Hoyt, and her brother, George lived on the other side. Zolah May, or May as she preferred to be called, also lived close by. Other than Hazel, Minnie had not seen Matt's oldest children since they were babies, and it was an incredible experience to see the adults they had become.

The ladies had so many plans for the three weeks Minnie and Ellen would be staying. They would be busy with day excursions, and occasionally stay in hotels along the way. Hazel and May took their mother, Minnie and Ellen to Virginia Beach, Yorktown and Williamsburg first. Seeing the Atlantic Ocean for the first time was a thrill for Ellen, and seeing so much rich American history was also a treat. The historical tour did not stop there, however. They also spent a few days visiting Washington, D.C.

Minnie and Matt had so much catching up to do and they enjoyed the quiet evenings together to reminisce and share family stories with Ellen, Hazel and May. Their days were busy, but they always made time to visit and share quality time with one another. Minnie loved being with her sister, just being able to reach out and touch her was too good to be true. She treasured every moment with her and thanked God for the opportunity to be with her once again. The time with Matt was going by much too fast for Minnie. She dreaded the day they would say goodbye, not knowing if she would ever see her sister again.

Minnie and the ladies were saving the best for last, and the day had finally come to meet up with Aunt Callie in Boone to tour the old stomping grounds. She could hardly wait to see her aunt, but was sad to think she would never see Uncle Tilden again.

They left early that morning. The car ride to Boone took hours, but it felt like only minutes. Minnie and Matt visited and reminisced all the way through Virginia and North Carolina. Before they knew it, they had arrived in Boone and were pulling up to Aunt Callie's home. Minnie could hardly wait to get out of the car and knock on her front door.

The ladies hurried out of the car and made their way to the front porch, when suddenly the door opened. There she stood, forty five years older, but the same little Aunt Callie. She was just as pretty and petite as ever. Minnie held her arms out to her and they embraced, trying to hold back the tears. Callie invited them inside, and Minnie introduced her to Ellen. It was a very special moment Minnie knew she would never forget.

"I always knew you'd come back, Minnie Lee," Callie said. "Well, it's about time!"

"I never thought I'd have the chance to come back, Aunt Callie. I just can't believe I am here with you and Matt both. I am just so happy to be here now," Minnie replied.

"I've missed you for a long time, dear. Your uncle missed you too."

Minnie gently held onto Callie's arm in a reassuring way. "I know, and I miss him too. I was so sad to get your letter about Uncle Tilden. I guess I just didn't make it back here soon enough."

The ladies visited and had coffee together for awhile longer. They had a lot of miles to cover that day, so they decided it was time to get started for Blowing Rock. First stop was the Cone Manor. It was a cool autumn day but pleasant enough for a drive through the Appalachian Mountains. The colors along the way were brilliant orange, yellow, brown and purple. The day was nearly perfect, if not for some drizzling rain and fog that was starting to settle in.

They traveled the Blue Ridge Parkway to milepost 294. The manor, which once had extensive orchards, gardens and livestock was now a museum for the public. Unfortunately, the manor was closed from fall until spring, and the ladies found the museum to be closed for the winter.

"We traveled all this way and it's closed? I can't believe this," Ellen said as she and Minnie stood outside of the locked gate looking in at the grand old majestic home. The stately manor was beautiful in the mist of the rain with the fog settling in the valley below. The colorful autumn colors surrounded the beautiful white Victorian-Colonial beauty for as far as they could see. Despite the dreary weather, it was beautifully stunning and grand. Ellen was very disappointed her grandmother would not be able to tour the manor.

"That's fine, Ellen. Just being here is what's important. It's still as beautiful as I remember it. I am glad we are here," Minnie reassured her granddaughter.

"Me too, grandma," Ellen replied.

Callie joined Minnie and Ellen at the iron gate. "Such fond memories. Tilden loved this place, and Arthur too. He took great pride in making sure this place was tip top."

"Where have the years gone?" Minnie replied. "Seems only yesterday I walked these grounds. Yet, it seems so very long ago. So much has happened in my life since those days."

Ellen took a few photos of the area, and then the ladies piled into the car and were on their way to Las Cruces.

Las Cruces was a small town that had not changed much in the years Minnie had been gone. Minnie found the small grocery store just as it was when she left more than forty years ago. The old cracker and pickle barrels setting in front was a scene lost in time.

Once inside, the memories rushed into Minnie's head. Even the familiar smell of the place brought back fond memories. Nothing had changed much, and this pleased Minnie. She was so happy they had stopped. An older man shopping in the store caught Minnie's eye. She was fairly sure she recognized him, but did not want to assume.

Could it really be Jake? Would he know her? Their chance meeting was an incredible act of fate.

Minnie walked up to the man and gently reached out to touch his arm.

"Are you Jake?" Minnie asked with a smile.

"Yes I am," the man said.

"You don't remember me, do you?" Minnie asked.

"No ma'm, I don't believe I do," the man said in a soft voice.

Minnie looked into his eyes, hoping he would eventually recognize something familiar about her.

"Jake, I'm Minnie Coffey," she replied.

Jake's mouth dropped open in disbelief, but then quickly he smiled and gave Minnie a hug.

"I am sorry I didn't recognize you. I never expected to see you in a million years! I can't believe I am standing here with you, Minnie. After all these years, how can this be? Why are you here?"

Minnie explained to Jake that she was visiting the area and traveling with her granddaughter. She introduced Ellen to Jake, and Callie and Matt said hello to the boy they remembered from many years ago. After a short visit, the ladies left the store to have lunch in a nearby café. A horse and wagon loaded down with tobacco just happened to stop at the restaurant just before the ladies went inside. Taking advantage of her opportunity, Ellen offered to buy a plug of tobacco from the driver to take home to her grandpa George. The kind farmer gave Ellen the tobacco without charge.

Once they had their meal, the ladies continued on with their tour, next stop was the Coffey family's old home on Shulls Mills road. They left the main highway and traveled on an old country road up in the hills outside of Blowing Rock. The ladies laughed and visited, sharing stories of their youth. Ellen enjoyed listening to them, and loved it that her grandma seemed so happy.

Finally they arrived at the old Coffey home site. What use to be a cleared field was now over grown with timber and brush. The grape arbor and the apple tree still stood amongst the roses, but the house was gone. The stone chimney had fallen into a heap where the house once stood. Minnie shared stories of her childhood with Ellen and pointed out places where she had played as a child. She pointed out where buildings had once stood, where they planted their garden and reminisced about how things once were. After a couple hours of walking around and viewing the property, they piled into the car and were off to visit John and Laura Moody.

When the car pulled up in front of the Moody's home, John and Laura were outside. Callie explained to them who Minnie was and they were pleasantly surprised that Minnie had returned to North Carolina after all these years. John and Laura were so happy to see Minnie again and so glad they had taken time out of their busy schedule to stop and visit them. Before they left, the Moodys gave them a bag of apples and they soon were on their way back to Boone to take Callie home.

Assuming she would never see Callie again, leaving her in Boone was very difficult and emotional for Minnie. However, she would not take the short time she was able to spend with her for all the money in the world. Sadly, their journey was nearly over in North Carolina and they were heading back to Ashland, Virginia. In a few days they would be boarding the train again and heading west for home. Minnie hated to leave, but she missed George and her family and knew it was time to go home.

Minnie thoroughly enjoyed her time with Matt and the three weeks went by much too quickly. The day had come for her and Ellen to catch the train for home. Minnie said a tearful goodbye to Matt, and Hazel drove her and Ellen back to the train station. She expressed her gratitude to Hazel and May for driving her and Ellen around during their three week stay. Their time with Matt and her daughters would always be three very memorable weeks in her life.

15 Changes

Soon Minnie and Ellen were home. George was happy to have his wife home again, and Minnie was happy to be with him. She enjoyed sharing her adventures and expressed how grateful she was for the opportunity to travel so far away to see her family again. George was very happy for Minnie and glad she was able to go "home" to visit.

A few weeks after they arrived home from their east coast adventure, Ellen and Minnie gathered together to look at photographs Ellen had taken of their trip. She had them developed in slide form, so Minnie and Ellen sat and viewed them through a slide show viewer and fondly reminisced and recollected their adventures.

"Often I've longed to go home," Minnie confessed. "But as much as I loved seeing the old place again, it only made me realize that this is my home and this is where I want to be. I am very blessed to be here and have my family around me."

Ellen smiled. She was happy knowing her grandmother felt that way. She knew how sad it would be to long for something you could never have. As difficult as Minnie's life was at times, it seemed to all work out for the best. In the autumn of her years, it was comforting to know that she was happy and content with the way her life had played out. Minnie would spend the rest of her days happy that her life was as it should have been, with no regrets. There was no doubt in her mind that her life should be any different than it was.

Although Candus passed away several years prior, Lee Cook still managed to keep in contact with the family. He played a pivotal roll in the family's success with moving to Okanogan County forty six years ago. Lee married twice more after Candus passed away, and died at the age of eighty six on October 18, 1957. Minnie's brother, Joe died on June 5, 1958 at the age of seventy one years old. Thirteen days later, her sister, Matt died on June 18, 1958.

Minnie and George's family began to expand to great grandchildren. Doris and Bob's son, Andy and his wife, Joan had Patty and Danny. Their son, Phil and wife, Joan had Larry, Diane and Doug. Their daughter, Lorraine and her husband, Bill Gilden had John, Jimmy, Terry and Jill.

Minnie lost George on December 7, 1962. He became sick while at home, and was taken to the hospital. While there, he suffered another stroke. This time, he was not as fortunate as he was with the first stroke in 1941. George died two days later, and suddenly Minnie was alone.

Dave and Leda purchased The Little Store on Warren Avenue in Pateros in 1964 and they sold groceries and gasoline. Leda took a job at the school working as a cook and they enjoyed a good life with young son, Perry. Ellen had married Herman Hixon in 1958 and they had daughter, Kathy born in 1959 and son, Kevin followed in 1964. Leda and Dave's son, David had gone into the army in 1958 and spent some time in Korea, but returned home and married Donna Vroman in 1961 and they also had two children, Aaron, born in 1962 and Dana in 1964.

By 1965 there were a lot of changes in the scenery of the area, in particular to the towns of Pateros and Entiat. The Douglas

County Public Utility District had plans for a new dam on the Columbia River just south of Pateros. A huge undertaking would soon take place, ending with the town of Pateros being destroyed in a major flood. The dam backed the water up and created a lake where Pateros once was. Homes on higher ground were spared, but the town and the homes nearer to the river all succumbed to the raging flood waters. Entiat was also consumed in the water backed up by the dam.

Minnie was forced to move, as were Dave and Leda. Their home, which was once Uncle Andy's beautiful Victorian style house, fell victim to the wrecking ball and eventually the flood waters. Minnie was also sad to lose her home, the home she had once shared with George. But no one had a choice in the matter. The law was on the side of the utility district. The town and properties were public domain, and it was futile to fight off the inevitable.

Dave and Leda purchased a home that sat higher up the hill on Dawson Street. The home, built in 1927 was once owned by Doctor Stout and his wife, Bernice. At one time, it served as their residence as well as their clinic. Ellen's first child, Kathy had her first well baby visit in this very house back in 1959. And now, Dave and Leda owned the old home. They purchased a mobile home for Minnie and set it on their property. Minnie had her own home again, but was living next door to her daughter if she ever needed anything. This made her feel secure but independent.

Minnie's siblings all preceded her in death. Larkin passed away in June of 1968. Minnie was the last of the original Coffey family who ventured west back in 1911. Often she thought of her family and their struggles to make a better life for themselves. She missed them all but cherished the precious memories she held deep in her heart. Amazingly enough, Minnie's Aunt Callie Isenhour lived to be one hundred years old and would not pass away until January 17, 1980. She died the same year that her seventy eight year old daughter, Francis passed.

On December 2, 1972 on a cool crisp afternoon, Minnie put on a pot of stew and then went out to her garden to pick the last of the cabbage for the season. Leda joined her in the garden awhile, and then the ladies parted ways, going to their respective homes. Minnie took a head of cabbage into her home and sat down in her large chair in the living room to rest while her favorite television program was on. Minnie gently fell asleep with the cabbage and the knife she used to cut the cabbage still lying across her lap, and quietly and peacefully passed away at eighty two years old.

Later that evening, her friend, Polly Gobat made several unsuccessful attempts to telephone Minnie. Sensing something might be wrong, Polly called Leda to check on her. Leda stepped out of her house and could see that Minnie's curtains were still open and there were no lights on. Leda's heart sunk. She knew she would find the worst. Minnie always pulled her curtains before dusk, and turned on her lights. It was obvious that something was terribly wrong. Leda found her mother in her favorite chair, the television still on, the cabbage and knife still in her lap and the stew scorched on the stove. As heartbroken as Leda was, she was comforted knowing her mother passed away so peacefully.

Her legacy lives on in all of us. The gentle woman responsible for us being here will never be forgotten. Her love of laughter, her strength of character, her love for life and her beautiful spirit will live on in all our hearts forever.

Minnie was my Great Grandma, Leda was my Grandma and Ellen is my mother. I write this story in tribute to them all, but I wanted to share the story of Minnie so that generations of Coffeys who come after her can appreciate her legacy and share this story with their children. I loved my Great Grandma Minnie dearly, I remember her fondly and I wish I could have had more time with her on this earth. I was thirteen years old when she left us and I was much too young to realize and appreciate what I had with her until it was lost forever.

Grandma Minnie would probably laugh and be embarrassed to know I've written a book in honor of her and her life, that's just the way she was. She was humble, quiet and unassuming. But I am proud of who I am and where I came from. She's a very important part of the legacy and the rich Brownlee – Coffey family history of Okanogan County that I now hand down to my sons, Sam and Tim.

Grandma Minnie grew nasturtiums every spring, so every year I plant nasturtium seeds in her honor. I thought it only fitting that this should be a part of the title of this tribute, because it was one of her favorite things to grow. Every spring when I drop a seed in the dirt, I think of her. When the plants peak through the surface of the dirt, I think of her. When they are in full bloom, I smile and think of her.

Minnie's legacy includes four daughters, Leda, Doris, Hazel and Grace. She had one son, John and three step sons, David, Walter and Robert. Her grandchildren, Ellen, David, Perry, Lorraine, Phil, Andy, Jean, Janice, Nancy, Jimmy, William, Lerin, Greg, Suzan, Marty and step grandchildren Wayne and Glen. Great grandchildren Kathy, Kevin, Aaron, Dana, Patty, Danny, Robin, Diane, Larry, Douglas, Rhys, Olivia, Maria, Lucas, Emily, Johnny,

Terry, Jimmy, Jill, Casey, Kellie, Amy, Amber, Kristen and Brandon. Step great grandchildren, Karen, Kathy, Keith, Michael and Kevin. Great great grandchildren, Teresa, Terry, Jason, Tiffanie, Torrie, Taylen, Drew, Ashley, Stacey, Mark, Samuel, Timothy, Nicholas, Ross, Justina, Torie, David John, Caroline, Orion, Carson, Jackson, Mateo, Jayden, Jake, Joey, Jessica, Catherine, Megan, Desirae, Rachael, Clint, Hannah, Clara, Scott, Robert, Natalie, Symarah, Austin, and Aubrey. Great great great grandchildren Henry Ray, Kendra, Simian, Stella, Keenan, Kade, Grace, Daniella, Lilyann and Kamryn.

I would be remiss if I did not mention my cousin, and Grandma Minnie's great grandson who valiantly gave his life while serving his country in Beirut, Lebanon on April 18, 1983. Terry Lee Gilden was a member of the 1st Special Forces Operational Detachment-Delta (Delta Force), and was killed protecting the ambassador at the time of the embassy bombing. Terry was born September 15, 1958. He left behind one daughter, Teresa and wife Mary.

There will be many generations to follow, and I hope they enjoy learning about the generations that came before them. There's an old Scottish saying, "Remember the men from whence you came." The Scots and the Irish both know how important families are, and they respect and appreciate those who came before to make it possible for us all to be here now.

THE END

www.ingramcontent.com/pod-product-compliance
Lightning Source LLC
Chambersburg PA
CBHW061259280526
45784CB00002B/817